Religious Liberty and Conscience

Also by Milton R. Konvitz

Religious Liberty and Conscience

A CONSTITUTIONAL INQUIRY

Milton R. Konvitz

THE VIKING PRESS

NEW YORK

VIKING COMPASS EDITION
Issued in 1969 by The Viking Press, Inc.
625 Madison Avenue, New York, N.Y. 10022

Distributed in Canada by
The Macmillan Company of Canada Limited

Library of Congress catalog card number: 68-31398

Printed in U.S.A.

To Horace M. Kallen,
   who speaks the words of secularism,
and to Leo Jung,
   who speaks the words of religion,
yet are the words of one and of the other
words of the Living God.

Preface

When looked at superficially, church-state relations in the United States can appear to be quite simple. The state may not interfere with religious liberty, and there is a constitutional separation of church and state. Therefore, there are, and there can be, no problems; indeed, infringements of religious liberty or church-state relations cannot occur in the United States.

But the facts are quite different. Few subjects are more complex or as likely to provoke deep emotion. And there seem to be no ultimate formulations or ultimate solutions.

For one thing, Americans are constantly changing their views about the proper province of the state. For example, until recently—perhaps the participation of Robert Frost in the inaugural ceremonies of President John F. Kennedy on January 20, 1961, could be taken as a point of departure—very few Americans thought that the government had a legitimate role in the furtherance of the fine arts, music, creative writing, the theater, and the humanities in general. The prevailing opinion was that action in these areas had to be strictly private, that the American people had not delegated to the federal or to state governments the power to act in these fields. Now, however, few question governmental interest and action in the stimulation of cultural concerns.

I cite this development simply as an example of the fact that the limits on the legitimate powers of government are not frozen. Lines are drawn, but they are constantly being redrawn, and no one can foretell where the line will be in the next decade or even in the next year.

A similar judgment may be made of religion. The interests and actions of religions have undergone radical changes, and the groups and their thought continue in motion. Churches—I use the term generically to include organized religions of all denominations and sects—today do things that were unthinkable a very short time ago. Our views about the very nature of religion, like our views of the state, have undergone drastic changes, and the end of this process is not in sight. We no longer know definitely the things that are Caesar's and the things that are God's.

The result is that questions of church-state relations, and of the reaches of the state, and of religion, and of conscience, have taken on degrees of complexity and delicacy for which we lack adequate conceptual equipment. We seem to have come out of the age of innocence; it is as if now, for the first time, we have tasted of the fruit of the tree of knowledge and are quite unprepared to discuss our predicament, let alone answer our questions.

In this book I propose to describe these developments and sketch, in broad strokes, some of the questions they have posed for us. I do not profess to have the answers; I am not sure that anyone has them today. I am not even sure that we really know how to ask the questions in a way that will disclose the reality, vitality, and consequences of the issues. But I have brooded on these questions for a long time; and I would like to think that it is not only the thoughts of youth that are long, long thoughts.

This book originated in the Paley Lectures in American Culture and Civilization that I had the privilege to deliver at the Hebrew University in Jerusalem in March 1968. I am deeply grateful to this great institution for the opportunity it afforded me to prepare and present the lectures, and to enjoy, as a fringe benefit, the opportunity once again to visit Israel and to renew old friendships and acquire new ones. I am thankful to many persons for countless acts of kindness—I can mention here only Dr. Nathan Rotenstreich, Rector of the University; Dr. Yoshua Arieli, Director of American Studies; and Dr. Edward Poznanski, until recently Academic Secretary. My other friends will need to consider themselves, as lawmen say, incorporated by reference.

I wish also to acknowledge gratefully my indebtedness to Aaron Asher, of The Viking Press, for his editorial encouragement and help that went beyond the call of duty.

M. R. K.

Cornell University
May 2, 1968

NOTES FOR THE VIKING COMPASS EDITION

I have taken advantage of the opportunity to update the discussion in several places in the text and footnotes. Because of exigencies of space, the following three newly added footnotes are printed here rather than on pages 62, 92, and 98 respectively.

Page 62: A recent case in which the court was restrictive in its view as to what is a religion is *United States v. Kuch*, 288 F. Supp. 439 (1968). The court looked for "solid evidence of a belief in a supreme being, a religious discipline, a ritual, or tenets to guide one's daily existence."

Page 92: In June 1967 Congress amended the military draft act by omitting reference to Supreme Being; but retained the requirement of "religious training and belief" and the exclusion of "essentially political, sociological, or philosophical views, or a merely personal moral code." 50 U.S.C. App. Sec. 456(j). The mere omission of Supreme Being while retaining intact the other requirements and exclusions has no effect on the line of thought developed in this chapter.

Page 98: On April 1, 1969, Judge Charles Wyzanski of the United States District Court in Boston upheld claim of John H. Sisson, who did not claim that he was a religious conscientious objector in the statutory sense. The court held that the act of Congress discriminated unconstitutionally against atheists and agnostics and others who, like Sisson, are motivated by "profound moral beliefs." See also annot. in 13 (U.S.) L. ed. 1189 (1965); *United States v. Schacter*, 37 LW 2350 (1968).

M.R.K.

May 11, 1969

Contents

Religious Liberty and Conscience

1. The New Look of the Church-State Problem

1

The world today is extremely complex, yet certain happenings seem to have universal sweep—industrialization seems to be everywhere sought after; urbanization, with or without industrialization, seems to be a strong force throughout the world. These are material forces that one can see and even measure.

There are also intellectual and spiritual forces at work throughout the world—the spread of literacy, which must go hand in hand with industrialization and urbanization, closing cultural gaps between city and country; equality of status for women, with universal suffrage and the right of women to education and to entry into professions and business.

But intellectually and spiritually, perhaps the most important phenomenon is the widespread mood of questioning which is not afraid to touch fundamental aspects of life and what had been stable aspects of social existence. The formerly monolithic Communist world has cracked: China and Russia have become enemies; the Iron Curtain has been lifted; some Communist countries in Eastern Europe have become, in varying degree, independent of the U.S.S.R.

We see a similar phenomenon when we look at the Roman Catholic Church. The Pope, regardless of the dogma of infallibility, no longer controls the minds and acts of Roman Catholics as he did in the past. Celibacy for priests and nuns, the prohibition of contraception and abortion, parochial education, exclusion of laymen from church service and church administration—these and other established dogmas are now openly questioned.

Another part of this picture is the universal questioning of the moral judgment. There is no doubt that in our time we have been witnessing a continuing revolution in sexual mores. What is important is not that there is more premarital and extramarital sexual activity than there was a hundred or fifty or ten years ago, but that attitudes have changed. It is no longer possible, as it had been for centuries, to preach the simple virtue of chastity. Today when one talks about chastity, one must do so critically, with the understanding that the question is open and that one's hearers are not ready to accept an absolute prohibition on sexual activity outside of marriage without question, as a law of God.

Now one finds this mood, though in varying degrees, at least throughout the Western world—in Europe, in North America, equally among Roman Catholics, Protestants, Jews, humanists, atheists, democratic peoples, Communists, and even among the people and priests of such countries as Spain.

And this questioning mood spares no one and nothing. It refuses to exempt God and religion. The "honest to god" debate started by the Bishop of Woolwich, and the "death of God" debate, and the "secular city" debate, and the debates in Vatican Council II—all are part of the same phenomenon: nothing, no institution, no one, and no belief is too sacred to be questioned. Today everyone comes from Missouri and demands to be shown.

This questioning mood, as it does not exclude the church or religion, does not exclude the state. We can no longer assume that citizens will automatically dance to whatever tune the government chooses to play. In the United States the struggle over civil rights, with its sit-ins and other forms of demonstrations, has shown that a state and its laws can be used for generations to fix and perpetuate institutions that are outrageously immoral. It no longer suffices to say to people: "It is the law. It is not for you and the likes of you to question the law. Obey the law and shut up!" Such talk is no longer respected. Millions of men and women know and say that the law may be shockingly immoral. And they can point to the laws of the Nazis, under which millions of Jews and other peoples were brutally murdered. They can point to the laws of the U.S.S.R., under which a tyrannical system has been imposed on hundreds of millions of men. They can point to the racist laws of Rhodesia and the Republic of South Africa. They can point even to the laws of Christian nations, such as those of Latin American countries, and the economic and social institutions of some Islamic countries, which perpetuate systems of rank social, sexual, and economic exploitation. Now, perhaps for the first time in history, the law as an institution is itself being critically, openly, defiantly challenged.

The war in Vietnam has to be seen in this context. The American people are deeply and widely divided over the war. Our young people are the most openly critical. They no longer are willing to accept the word of the President without question. They raise *moral* questions about a situation that previously would have been considered exclusively political or military. Our young people no longer accept the motto: "My country, right or wrong!" They no longer accept the advice: "Yours not to reason why. Yours but to do and die." They say that if they are called upon to die, they have a right and perhaps a duty to ask why.

Now, unfortunately, it is our young people who experience most keenly the shaking of our foundations. It is they who are subject to the draft and are called upon to fight in a war the morality of which many of them question. It is they who are called upon to be sexually chaste at a time when the morality of chastity is being openly questioned—and at a time when the means of birth control are more readily available and efficient than ever before; when sexuality is more openly exploited in books, movies, fashion, news, and advertising than ever before; when more young people are away from home at campuses than ever before; when young people have more money to spend than they ever before had; when opportunities for sexual relations are greater than ever before; and at a time when they are least likely to look to their religion and its spokesmen for authoritative answers. They may go to clergymen for counseling and guidance, but not for dogmatic answers. Perhaps no generation of young people in the past has faced so many temptations, so many difficult problems, with so little opportunity for traditionally happy solutions.

All this is only a part of the background against which we need to see what has been happening in our own time to affect the traditional relations between church and state. These relations are being radically changed. The federal Elementary and Secondary Education Act of 1965 is the most obvious instance of this change. We do not by any means know what the ultimate resolution of the changes will be. We even lack the proper critical framework within which to structure and evaluate the changes. But still, we are not exempt from detecting the changes and from tentatively and cautiously charting their possible future course. The changes are the result of new material forces in our society, of discontent and disillusionment, of an eagerness for new institutions and new conceptions and ideals that would more closely reflect the material, intellectual, and spiritual conditions of men in the world today.

2

In looking more closely at the picture of recent church-state relations in the United States, much stress should be put on the election of John F. Kennedy as President in November 1960. As far as we know, he was not elected merely by his coreligionists. Roughly speaking, the alignment was liberals vs. conservatives (a larger proportion of traditionally liberal Jews, for example, than of Roman Catholics voted for him) and the significant thing was that *it was liberals, generally fearful of the Roman Catholic role in national politics, who elected Kennedy,* the first Roman Catholic to occupy the White House. Kennedy shattered an old image, and perhaps did so for all time. The change was not of principle, but of action: some thirty-four million Americans went to the polls and voted for a church-going Roman Catholic. Church-state relations in the United States could never again be the same after that event.

There is considerable irony in the success of Kennedy. The liberals voted for him, despite his Catholicism, because they believed him when he said that, as President, he would make his decisions in accordance with what his conscience would tell him to be the national interest and without regard to religious dictates or pressures, and furthermore, that he believed in an America "where the separation of church and state is absolute." But his election contributed immeasurably to the forces that were to shatter the image of the Irish Catholic in the United States and to relax the tension of the separation of church and state, so that it may never again be as absolute as it was at the time of Kennedy's election. Kennedy was on record as opposing any federal aid to parochial schools, yet his election can be seen as one of the essential conditions that prepared President Johnson, Congress, and the American people for the provisions in the Elementary and Secondary Education Act of 1965, which weaken, if they do not violate, the principle of separation of church and state.

The personality and work of Pope John XXIII and the work of Vatican Council II have resulted in fundamental changes in the Roman Catholic Church, in the attitudes of Roman Catholics, and in the way others now see the Church. There are many aspects of this complex phenomenon; for our purposes one can select a few recent developments. Especially interesting are those that affect the position of the Church regarding the Bible, for here the Church has made some changes that are bound to have deep effects on church-state attitudes and practices in the United States.

Historically, the Church has not placed primary emphasis on the Bible. The position of the Church has been that the Church itself stands as the center of Christianity—the Church which, the Church says, was founded by Jesus, who named Peter the first Bishop of Rome, who, therefore, became the first Pope. According to Roman Catholic beliefs, it is tradition —as maintained and transmitted by the Church—that determines the character of Christianity. It is tradition, with the Church as its carrier and guardian, that determines the place, role, and meaning of the Bible. The Church has never been Bible-centered; and in its reading of the Bible, it has never been fundamentalist. The Bible must be interpreted by the priests (the Church); the Bible does not speak directly to every man; the Bible speaks through the Church, its priests and its traditions.

This was a fundamental cause of the Reformation. The early reformers contended that the Church stood as too high a wall between the Bible as the word of God and mankind to whom the word was spoken. The Reformation was many things. It was a social as well as a religious revolution, but first and foremost it was a back-to-the-Bible movement (though not strictly "back," since the Bible had never been the "rock" on which Jesus was supposed to have built his house).

As a consequence, the Church never encouraged Catholics to read the Bible for themselves, and so it stood in the way of translations into the vernacular. A by-product of this position was that for centuries literacy was limited to churchmen; and even today literacy is relatively low in Catholic countries outside of North America and Western Europe. The Church persecuted Christian scholars who undertook to translate the Bible—the Oxford priest John Wycliffe, for example, who wanted the Bible to reach the people directly, without priestly intermediaries, and therefore translated the New Testament and part of the Hebrew Scriptures. He died after a paralytic stroke in 1384, but he was posthumously condemned at the Council of Constance in 1415, and his body was disinterred, burned, and thrown into the River Swift. When Tyndale's English New Testament was published on the Continent and copies were brought into England in 1526, churchmen publicly burned the copies at Paul's Cross. When the churchmen caught up with Tyndale on the Continent, he was imprisoned for sixteen months, then strangled and burned at the stake.

The Catholic Church finally consented to the preparation of a translation of the Bible into English. This was the Douay Version, published in France in 1610; but it was prepared by priests, with an eye on Church dogma and teachings. Catholics were banned from using the King James Version, which was based on Tyndale's translation.

When Pope John XXIII decided to try to establish some bridges between the Church and the "separated brethren," he knew that the Church would first of all be required to rethink its position with respect to the Bible, the center of Protestant Christianity. The conservatives at the Vatican were opposed, but Pope John threw his weight behind the liberals.

We do not know how Vatican Council II would have resolved this fundamental issue had Pope John lived several more years. Under Pope Paul VI what the Council did respecting the Bible can best be described as a compromise that reflects the strong weight of the conservative wing; but it made some concessions, significant enough to change radically the relations between the Church and Protestantism.

In the document *Dogmatic Constitution on Divine Revela-*

tion (1965) the Council reaffirmed its traditional stand. In reading and interpreting the Bible, said the Council, "the living tradition of the whole Church must be taken into account. . . . For all of what has been said about the way of interpreting Scripture is subject finally to the judgment of the Church, which carries out the divine commission and ministry of guarding and interpreting the word of God." [1] In the *Decree on Ecumenism* (1964) the Council refers to the Protestant attitude toward the Bible approvingly yet critically: "A love, veneration, and near cult of the sacred Scriptures lead our brethren to a constant and expert study of the sacred text." [2] This is both to compliment and to condemn.

> But when Christians separated from us affirm the divine authority of the sacred Books, they think differently from us— different ones in different ways—about the relationship between the Scriptures and the Church. In the Church, according to Catholic belief, an authentic teaching office plays a special role in the explanation and proclamation of the written word of God. Nevertheless, in dialogue itself, the sacred utterances are precious instruments in the mighty hand of God for attaining that unity which the Savior holds out to all men.[3]

What this means is that the Church continues to claim that it, and not the Bible, is the source of Christian teaching; that it alone has authority to interpret and to proclaim the teaching of the Bible. The Bible, however, may serve somehow as a basis of dialogue between the Church and the separated brethren. Since it is sacred and precious to all Christians, the Bible—says the Church—may prove to be a unifying instrument in the hands of God.

The largest concession was made regarding translations of the Bible. In the document on *Revelation*, the Council stated: "Easy access to sacred Scripture should be provided for all the Christian faithful. . . ." [4] This is perhaps the most novel and radical statement in the entire document. Never before had the Church urged the availability of the Bible for all Christians.

The document does not, however, open the door to the admission of all translations. The Church wants "suitable and correct translations." The document adds: "And, if given the opportunity and approval of Church authority, these translations are produced in cooperation with the separated brethren as well, all Christians will be able to use them." [5] This was the first time in history that the Church opened the door to the possibility of reviewing and accepting a translation prepared by non-Catholic, erstwhile heretic scholars.

Furthermore, the document called on Catholic clergy and on *all Christians* to read the Bible, to "put themselves in touch with the sacred text itself," whether through liturgy that uses the language of the Bible, or through devotional reading, or through special instruction and aids; but prayer should accompany the reading of the Bible, "so that God and man may talk together. . . ." [6]

In accord with these decisions of the Council, in 1965 the Roman Catholic hierarchy of England approved a Catholic edition of the Revised Standard Version, which had been produced by the (Protestant) National Council of Churches of Christ in 1946 and 1952. In May 1966 Richard Cardinal Cushing, Archbishop of Boston, gave official approval to the Oxford Annotated Bible with the Apocrypha, which uses the text of the Revised Standard Version. In November 1966 Pope Paul VI directed the Secretariat for Christian Unity, headed by Augustin Cardinal Bea, to plan cooperation with Protestant Bible groups for the production of common translations of the Bible and for their distribution. Cardinal Bea appointed the Reverend Walter M. Abbott, an American Jesuit scholar, to direct this work, and in November 1966 Father Abbott addressed the advisory council of the American Bible Society in New York.

This last detail is especially noteworthy because in the nineteenth century four Popes had condemned the work of the Protestant Bible societies. For example, Pope Leo XII in 1824 issued an encyclical, *Ubi Primum*, in which he condemned in strong language vernacular translations of the Bible prepared by Protestant groups. "It is to be feared," he said, "that by false interpretation the Gospel of Christ will become the gospel of men, or, still worse, the gospel of the devil."

Catholic canon law requires that all Bibles be published with notes, to make sure that what the Church considers the right interpretation shall be conveyed to the reader. Protestant Bible societies, on the contrary, have distributed editions of the Bible without notes, on the assumption that the word of the Bible can speak directly to every man without any interpositions. Now both parties are moving toward a middle ground: the inclusion of "noncontroversial" notes that will make the Bible intelligible where it may be difficult.

In agreeing with Protestants on a common Bible, the Roman Catholic Church had also to deal with the great problem presented by the Protestant exclusion of the Apocryphal books from their text of Sacred Scripture. The Protestants always translated and published separately the writings known as the Apocrypha, while the Catholics distributed these writings throughout their Bible. When the Revised Standard Version was prepared, the board of translators of the National Council of Churches undertook to translate the Apocrypha only at the request of the Protestant Episcopal Church, which, among Protestant denominations, has the closest affinities with the Roman Catholic Church. Thus, for centuries, Protestants and Catholics had significantly different Bibles, and until several years ago it was unthinkable that the Church would ever dare to make the great leap from the Douay Version of 1610 to the Oxford Annotated Bible of the Revised Standard Version of the National Council of Churches of Christ in America. The leap has occurred, and it is breathtaking, one of the most dramatic acts in the history c religion.*

* In June 1968 the United Bible Societies, a federation representing 35 Protestant groups, and the Vatican Secretariat for Promoting Christian

3

What do these events mean in terms of American church-state relations? If we look closely at the scene, we will observe that a great shifting of forces seems to have taken place.

The American public school had always been a stronghold of the Protestants, who with the exception of the Lutherans, never undertook to build church schools on any significant scale. Protestants were satisfied to include Protestant prayer, Protestant hymn-singing, and Protestant Bible-reading among public-school activities. Roman Catholics would not join in such prayers or hymns, nor could they listen to or read from the King James Version of the Bible. The Jews had even stronger grounds for objection to public-school prayers and Bible-reading. Jews and Catholics would attack these Protestant school practices in the courts, alleging that they breached the wall of separation between church and state and infringed on the religious liberty of non-Protestant pupils and their parents.

But while Jews and Catholics agreed in their objections to this Protestant misuse of the public schools, they pursued different courses of action. The Jews accepted the public school and supported it as a great educational and equally great unifying force in American society. They supported all efforts to improve the school system on all levels. Wherever possible, the Jews tried to keep religion out of the schools, or at least to keep religious practices down to a minimum. At the same time, the Jews built and maintained a network of Jewish religious schools that took the children late in the afternoon, after the public-school day was over. There were, until recently, very few Jewish

---

Unity published guidelines for the production of a Bible to serve both Protestants and Catholics. The apocryphal writings will be published in a separate section between the Old and New Testaments. There will be descriptive but no doctrinal notes, and there will be no comments on controversial passages.

all-day schools,[7] and until 1928, when Yeshiva University was founded, there was no Jewish sectarian college. The reason for this development is that Jews in general have a positive attitude to what Christians call secular interests and activities: they accept approvingly what Christians tend to dismiss as secular. Accordingly, "secularism," a pejorative term to many Christians, has a neutral position in Jewish thought and feeling. American Jews had, therefore, no hesitation in accepting the American public school as an important part of their lives as Americans and Jews. Because of their non-Christian attitude toward the secular, Jews never felt that the public school would be "godless" if the schools discontinued Bible-reading, prayers, and hymn-singing.

The Roman Catholic attitude was quite different. Of course Catholics resented and objected to Protestant dominance in the public-school system. Moreover, the Catholic Church found it impossible to legitimize any aspect of education that was not under Catholic clerical control; no part of education had a right to be secular and independent of Church influence. While to the Jew the secular, as part of God's creation, could participate in the sacred, to the Catholic what was not sacerdotally sanctioned might be sinfully secular and was therefore prohibited. It was, therefore, natural that the Catholic Church in the United States should build its own system of education, one that would tend to exclude all non-Catholic schools as off limits.

The first Catholic parish school was opened in 1810 at Emmitsburg, Maryland. By 1840 there were some two hundred such schools in the United States. In 1884 the Catholic hierarchy, at the Third Plenary Council in Baltimore, required that a school be built near every parish church unless the local bishop granted a dispensation, and declared that parents must send their children to Catholic schools.

The Church took the position that Catholic schools must be Catholic in every possible way: in content of courses, in methods of instruction, in the dress of the teachers, in the strict separation of the sexes, in attitudes and atmosphere—and that these rules applied to all schools and all classes and classrooms, from kindergarten through college and professional and graduate schools, from physical education through mathematics and the sciences; nothing was to be left out of the reach of Church influence and direction.[8] The result was a system of schools and colleges and universities that seemed foreign and strange to those on the outside. They were thought of as divisive, and by many as somehow subversive of American culture, as "un-American."

By 1968 there were, in the United States, 305 Catholic colleges with 434,000 students (not including seminaries, of which there were 437, with 40,000 seminarians); 1407 high schools, with 695,000 students; 868 private high schools, with 394,000 students; 10,375 elementary schools, with 4,089,000 students; 382 private elementary schools, with 75,678 students. In these colleges and schools there were more than 206,000 full-time teachers, teaching close to six million students.

No one can look at these figures without a feeling of respect for the devotion and generosity of the Catholic community in the United States.

4

But today we see that Roman Catholic attitudes have changed both toward their own parochial schools and toward the public school—and toward religion in the public school. As a consequence of these changes one can see as well an alteration in non-Catholic attitudes toward the Catholic school and also toward religious exercises and religious teaching in the public school.

In 1966 two important accounts of Catholic education appeared, the Greeley-Rossi study at the University of Chicago and the Notre Dame study, both supported by the Carnegie Corporation.[9] These and other books—especially *Are Parochial Schools the Answer?* by Mary Perkins Ryan—underscore the cry that has been heard almost everywhere among Catholics that the parochial schools must be radically modernized, that their doors and windows must be opened to let in fresh thought and light, that clerical control of the schools must be reduced and laymen and parents allowed to share in the direction of the schools, and that even the religious teaching in these schools, which the critics have found to be backward and ineffective, must be brought up to date. Because of the great increase in parochial school enrollment in recent years (between 1940 and 1960 the rate was more than double that of the public schools), the Church has been unable to supply enough teachers from the religious orders, with the result that in 1963 some thirty per cent of the teachers—65,000 in number—were lay teachers, an increase of almost 600 per cent in the last ten years of lay high school teachers and 169 per cent of lay elementary school teachers. These lay teachers, unlike the religious, receive salaries, and the salaries are often about half of those paid by the public schools. Both school systems compete for teachers, and the differential in pay has put the parochial schools at a great disadvantage. It has been estimated that by 1968–1969 the Catholic schools will take in a million more students than there were in 1962–1963. For this increased enrollment, the schools would need more than 20,000 additional religious and more than 10,000 additional lay teachers. New school construction would cost over $700 million. Today the parochial schools accommodate only forty-three per cent of all Catholic children of school age, a drop of five per cent in ten years; the schools are turning away about twenty per cent of all those who apply for admission. It has also become apparent that because of this selectivity the parochial school's pupils are by no means inferior in academic achievement and intellectual capacity. But overcrowding, the teacher shortage, heavy teaching loads, and limited budgets have placed on the schools an insufferably heavy burden. There is a recognized need for new, properly equipped science laboratories, and qualified science and mathematics teachers; for more foreign language instruction; for more modern textbooks; and for teaching that would be less saturated with religious ideas. The studies also show that the tendency today is to purchase the same textbooks that are used in the public schools in the teaching of mathematics, the sciences, and social studies, and to reduce the number of Church-dominated books. There are insistent demands for more educational experimentation, more open discussions of public and even religious issues, more academic freedom for the teacher and for the pupil, less regimentation and more personal involvement and expression. Taken together, these trends amount to a rejection of the enclosed, ghetto-like, separatist atmosphere of the Catholic schools and a promise to make them more like the better public schools, and even to surpass them in excellence.

The Greeley-Rossi study and Mary Perkins Ryan's book also disclose that *religious* teaching in the Catholic schools has not been very effective. This teaching, they say, has been virtually wasted on a majority of the students. These conclusions are supported by data such as the following: of Catholics with no parochial school education sixty-four per cent attend Mass on Sunday. The figure rises to only seventy-three per cent for those with some Catholic education, and to eighty-six per cent for those with total Catholic education. It appears, then, that the Catholic schools may not be absolutely essential for the survival of the Catholic religion. The studies also show that Catholic education makes some difference only if at least one of the child's parents is himself religiously observant. Thus the Chicago study concludes that Catholic education is virtually wasted on most of the pupils in the Catholic schools because of the absence of a sufficiently religious home environment, and Mrs. Ryan concludes that parochial schools are the least efficient and the most costly way to provide religious education. The Chicago study also shows that a Catholic with sixteen years of education in non-Catholic schools participates more in church sacraments than a Catholic with eight years of Catholic education—in other words, the amount of education a person receives may be more important than simply the amount of *religious* education.

The winds of criticism have also hit the Catholic colleges and universities. Many of the colleges, especially a substantial number of girls' schools, have been condemned as inferior and as unworthy of survival. The recent crisis at St. John's University, which erupted over differences between faculty and administration, was only the most serious and visible of many such struggles: Catholic college and university faculty members are demanding the same degree of academic freedom that exists in major secular American universities. Some Catholic colleges and universities are becoming secular. The boards that control some of these institutions have changed their bylaws to include lay trustees and even non-Catholic members. Protestant and Jewish scholars have been appointed to important chairs and to deanships in leading Catholic institutions of higher learning, and even to some chairs in Catholic seminaries. Today people on campuses no longer stare when they see women in religious garb walking about singly, or with coeds in mini skirts. Formerly Catholic priests would not preach in our so-called nondenominational university chapels, but today priests alternate at the pulpit with Protestant ministers and with rabbis. When we look at the scene in our cities and towns, away from the jurisdiction of the gown, we know that it is no longer a seven-day wonder when a Catholic priest preaches in a Protestant church or in a Jewish temple, and Catholic congregations are now participating in joint services with Protestants and Jews. In some communities priests have now joined the local ministerial organizations.

These and many other changes are all evidence of the American Catholic's response to the call of Pope John XXIII for an *aggiornamento*, for bringing the Church up to date. A most dramatic manifestation of this process is the highly visible activity of Catholic priests and nuns in the civil-rights and peace movements, which reflects a radical change in the nature of the Catholic priesthood and in the way the Church and its religious orders are seen by the rest of the nation.

Just as Catholics today are changing their views about their own parochial school system, they are also changing their views about the public school. Although for a century and a half they attacked Bible-reading and prayer in the public school as Protestant denominational forms of worship, Catholics today are among the strongest proponents of these practices. There has been a complete reversal of roles.

Although at first Protestants attacked the Supreme Court decisions in 1962 and 1963 banning the Regents' Prayer and Bible-reading in the public schools,[10] as the heat of passion was replaced by the light of understanding, national Protestant church groups veered over to the position of the Court. Thus, the United Presbyterian Church has come out publicly and firmly against all religious observances in public schools, and has in addition declared that in its view "Bible reading and prayers as devotional acts tend toward indoctrination of meaningless ritual and should be omitted. . . ." It should be noted that the objection is not merely on constitutional grounds but on *religious* grounds as well. So, too, the National Study Conference on Church and State of the National Council of Churches, which was attended by more than three hundred representatives of thirty-one leading Protestant denominations, stated that "Christians should welcome the decisions," which are, they said, "far from being anti-religious." Christians, they said, "do not believe that the question of authentic religion can ever be decided by formal rites and words alone. . . . In addition, the decisions are consistent with our concern for the religious liberty of all men." One could cite other evidence of the radical change in the position of leading Protestant bodies, which recognize frankly that the public school had been the captive of the Protestant churches, and now, following the lead of the Supreme Court, plead with their members to relinquish the power they had usurped, and give the public school to *all* the taxpayers, to whom it rightfully belongs: to Catholics, Jews, Unitarians, agnostics, atheists, and those with other varieties of religious beliefs or nonbeliefs.

The Catholic Church, however, has continued to attack the Supreme Court opinions and maintains that the public school must find accommodation for so-called neutral prayers and for devotional reading of the Bible.

What is the explanation for these radical developments? One can offer a number of reasons:

As we saw, Catholic doctrine had been opposed to individual Bible-reading not under the watchful eye and ear of the priest. But Vatican Council II has modified this position; moreover, the Church has agreed with the Protestants on a common Bible. There is, therefore, no longer any religious ground for objecting to the reading of the Bible in the public school.

Although the traditional Catholic position had been that there is no such thing as a neutral prayer, for only the priest could say what is and what is not a proper Catholic prayer, since Vatican Council II the practice, if not the principle, has been changed, and Catholics now join in common prayer with Protestants and Jews. The religious objection to a neutral prayer, such as that prepared by the Regents of the State of New York, no longer obtains. Why not, therefore, they ask, let the school children recite nondenominational prayers in their public-school classrooms?

There remains, of course, the constitutional objection to these devotional practices. But the American hierarchy has consistently argued that the Court misinterpreted and misapplied the Constitution in cases in which the Court affirmed the principle of separation of church and state. The Catholic Church in the United States has consistently denied the absoluteness of the principle of separation. This is still the position of the Church, as it must be if it is to continue to insist that parochial schools are entitled to support from tax funds for at least some aspects of their program. The logic seems to be something like this: If the public schools do not violate the principle of separation by engaging in certain religious practices, why should parochial schools be unconstitutionally deprived of public money because there is religious teaching in them? In other words, religious instruction or observance should not be a kiss of constitutional death for *any* school, whatever its ownership or sponsorship.

The Catholic Church is now reconciled to the fact that in the years ahead its schools will be able to accommodate only fifty per cent or less of the Catholic children of school age. Perhaps a majority of them will need to attend public schools. Although in 1884 the Church could say that "all Catholic parents are bound to send their children" to the parish (parochial) school unless the bishop permitted them to do otherwise, such a rule is no longer necessary or desirable. The public school should, therefore, become a proper school for Catholic children. *For this it is necessary that somehow God and religion become identified with the public school.* To this end, Bible-reading and common prayers may make a contribution, so that these schools may not be "godless" places.

Although it was fitting and proper in 1929 for Pope Pius XI, in his encyclical "The Christian Education of Youth," to say that to be a fit place for Catholic students, "it is necessary that all its teaching and the whole organization of the school, and its teachers, syllabi, and textbooks in every branch, be regulated by the [Catholic] Christian spirit," this is no longer acceptable. Catholic schools may, and now do, use secular textbooks in such subjects as social studies, the sciences, mathematics, and foreign language instruction. Thus the wall of separation between the sacred and the secular in education has been breached. Furthermore, the Catholic schools must, as we have seen, rely more and more on lay teachers, many of whom may not even be members of the Church. It is only a short step from these concessions to the idea of shared time, which permits the parochial school children to go over to the public school for courses in the sciences, mathematics, the manual arts, and certain other subjects. This principle was written into the Elementary and Secondary Education Act of 1965 with the approval of the Church and with at least the tacit approval of some leading Protestant and Jewish groups.

The 1965 act of Congress shows that large sections of Protestant and Jewish opinion have veered in the direction of favor for the parochial schools of the Catholic Church and for Jewish all-day schools. A Gallup Poll in 1963 showed that forty-four per cent were opposed to federal aid in the parochial schools; but only two years before, a similar poll showed that fifty-seven per cent had been opposed. It is safe to anticipate that the opposition will continue to decrease.

Bitter mutual suspicion and prejudice deriving from religious differences is on the wane. Not to go back to the nineteenth century, when America was plagued with the Know-Nothings and the Ku Klux Klan and other anti-Catholic, anti-Irish, and anti-immigration groups, and when Catholics, too, were wary of the Protestants and mistrusted everyone but coreligionists, but to go back only less than two decades, we can measure the distance that has been covered to bring closer the Catholics and their "separated brethren." In 1965 Congress passed the federal aid to education act with scarcely a murmur within or outside the Capitol. When, however, the Barden Bill was before Congress in 1949–1950, and Mrs. Eleanor Roosevelt came out with a mild, ladylike statement in favor of the bill and its prohibition of the use of federal funds for parochial schools, Cardinal Spellman publicly attacked and insulted her. Or one might compare instructively the anti-Catholic campaign against Alfred E. Smith when he ran for President in 1928 with the atmosphere that prevailed in 1960 when John F. Kennedy was a candidate.

In the last several years an important contribution to the more wholesome climate of opinion in this area has been made by our awareness of the fact that it was the Americans at Vatican Council II who urged the strongest possible statement on religious freedom. The *Declaration on Religious Freedom*, adopted by the Council in December, 1965, can be considered one of the most important events of the past two thousand years in the struggle for liberty. This statement, which is discussed more fully below, in Chapter Four, places the strongest emphasis on conscience and its rights. "On his part," says the declaration, "man perceives and acknowledges the imperatives of the divine law through the mediation of conscience." Note that the mediation is of conscience and not of any church or priest. "In all his activity," the declaration continues, "a man is bound to follow his conscience, in order that he may come to God, the end and purpose of life. It follows that he is not to be forced to act in a manner contrary to his conscience." The declaration then draws the following conclusion from these premises: "Nor, on the other hand, is he to be restrained from acting in accordance with his conscience, especially in matters religious." Of the 2391 prelates who participated in the Council, only seventy-five raised their voices in dissent from this declaration. This nearly unanimous action by the Church takes an impressively strong, principled position in favor of liberty of conscience and religious freedom.

Finally, Catholic and all other parents in the United States are greatly disturbed by the unrest of the young and by the evidence of a revolt against traditional morality and especially sexual mores. The moral foundations of society and of the family seem to be shaking. In the face of this development, many Americans—Catholics, Protestants, Jews, and persons without any religious affiliations—believe that perhaps religious education may help give the young a feeling for tradition, for roots in a spiritual heritage. Catholics traditionally have maintained that religion is indispensable for character formation and for grounding of moral principles. This is one of the reasons why they now contend for religion in the public schools—for the Catholic children and for all other children. This is a reason, too, why so many non-Catholic parents, even some who had never before had any interest in religious education, have developed a friendly regard for parochial schools, in which, they hope, the atmosphere would be conducive to instill in children a sense of moral and spiritual values. Thus, there has taken place a convergence of forces from different directions: Catholics and non-Catholics who would like to see some religion in the public schools, and non-Catholics and Catholics who wish to see the parochial schools strengthened and improved and perhaps even become models of excellence.

The relatively new socio-religious scene in the United States provides a setting that makes questions with respect to specific church-state situations harder to answer. For the new context makes it more difficult to see a sharp line between religious and nonreligious interests. The lines have become blurred. God and Caesar are no longer on totally opposite sides.

In a way, and paradoxically, this development—of which there are many other facets that we have not touched on—brings American society closer to the traditional Jewish position, which has refused to separate sharply the secular and the sacred, God and the world.

This problem of religion *versus* the secular, or of religion *and* the secular, or of religion defined as broad enough to incorporate the secular, will, in one way or another, trouble us.[11] It will be especially troublesome when we consider the fact that the First Amendment speaks of religion but not of conscience. Does conscience, when it does not profess to be religious, have the right to the same freedom that religion can claim? Or to put the question another way: Does the secular conscience enjoy the same constitutional status and dignity as that enjoyed by religion? A subordinate but also significant question is whether personal religion, that of the solitary man outside of any church or synagogue, is equally embraced by the First Amendment with religion in its institutional forms?

To consider these and related issues, we shall need to ask questions in the following order:

What is religion? Is it possible to formulate a definition without seriously hurting the spirit of the First Amendment?

Does the First Amendment protect nonreligion and atheism along with religion? Is it possible to protect religion without at the same time protecting, to the same degree, nontheistic and even antitheistic beliefs?

Does the Constitution protect conscience when it professes to be nonreligious?

At one time—and that not so very long ago—freedom of religion in the United States meant whatever satisfied Protestant wants and expectations. Later, as Roman Catholics and then Jews won for themselves respectability and power, Christianity was substituted for Protestantism, and then in turn the Judeo-Christian tradition displaced Christianity as representative of the American consensus. At the inauguration of John F. Kennedy, for the first time on such an occasion, an Eastern Orthodox clergyman participated in the ceremonies alongside a Roman Catholic priest, a rabbi, and a Protestant minister—as if to say: *All* religions have equal dignity and equal status.

The process is one of continuous, endless expansion and inclusion. Now, as we shall see, nontheistic, humanistic, secularistic, and atheistic religions clamor for and demand entry into and full membership in a covenant envisioned as radically pluralistic. This process raises, however, some fundamental questions about the very meaning of the term "religion" and of the Religion Clauses of the First Amendment—problems that will concern us in the chapters that follow.

2. *What Is Religion?*

1

Although it no longer seems startling that respected theologians seriously discuss a death-of-God theology, most people assume that this phenomenon is somehow part of that odd corner of the world inhabited by hippies, Communists, and other subversive, underworld characters—and that it is something altogether new. Yet, nearly two centuries ago, a Religion of Reason for a time became the established religion of France.

In 1793, during the later stages of the Revolution, under the leadership of Pierre Gaspard Chaumette, general prosecutor and leader of the Commune of Paris, the church of Notre Dame became the Temple of Reason. Sunday was abolished as the Sabbath and was replaced with a festival every tenth day. On November 10, 1793, in compliance with a proclamation by the Mayor of Paris, a Festival of Liberty and Reason was celebrated at the Temple, in which the symbols of Christianity had been covered and symbols of the new religion erected. In the nave a mountain had been constructed; on it stood a small Greek temple dedicated to Philosophy and adorned on the sides by busts of celebrated philosophers. A torch of Truth burned before the altar of Reason. One of the officials read the Declaration of the Rights of Man and Citizen, which had been adopted as the Preamble to the Constitution of 1791. Someone delivered a moral sermon, after which music was played. The central event was the entry of a young woman, on other days an actress of the Paris Opera, on this occasion the goddess or personification of Liberty. Dressed in red, white, and blue, she was carried into the Temple on a chair entwined with ivy and borne by four citizens. Other young girls, costumed in white and crowned with roses, preceded and followed the goddess of Liberty. The spectators rendered homage to her by stretching out their arms and singing a hymn:

> Come, holy Liberty, inhabit this temple,
> Become the goddess of the French people.

Then busts, including one of the recently assassinated Marat, were carried in, and following them, a procession of musicians and soldiers of the Republic. After more hymns and speeches, the people left the Temple and went to the Convention, where Chaumette spoke as follows:

Legislators! Fanaticism has given way to reason. Its bleared eyes could not endure the brilliancy of the light. This day an immense concourse has assembled beneath those Gothic vaults, which for the first time re-echoed the truth. There the French [people] have celebrated the only true worship, that of Liberty, that of Reason. There we have formed wishes for the success of the arms of the Republic. There we have abandoned inanimate [Christian] idols for Reason, for that animated image [man], the masterpiece of Nature.

As he uttered these words, the speaker pointed to the goddess of Reason, who then received a fraternal kiss from the President, as the audience cried out: "The Republic forever! Reason forever! Down with fanaticism!" Members of the Convention then joined the audience in a processional return to the Temple of Reason for still more patriotic hymns.[1]

This cult of Brumaire lasted hardly a year. Robespierre crushed it, and Chaumette died on the guillotine at the age of thirty-one. But Robespierre did not re-establish the Catholic Church. On June 8, 1794, he initiated the cult of the Supreme Being, and this too was accomplished with great pomp. The decree establishing the cult stated that the French people recognize the existence of the Supreme Being and the immortality of the soul, and that the cult worthy of the Supreme Being is the practice of the duties of man. The Convention, under the influence of Robespierre, gave official recognition to the Supreme Being, and decreed a Festival of the Supreme Being to replace the Festival of Reason. Robespierre walked at the head of the procession on the day of the festival, carrying flowers and wheatears in his hand, to the sound of chants and hymns. There was a great wagon drawn by milk-white oxen; in front of the cart were sheaves of golden grain, and in the back shepherds and shepherdesses posed to make a rustic scene. "The whole mummery," a nineteenth-century Englishman wrote, "was pagan." It was, he added, "the most disgusting and contemptible anachronism in history." For how, he asked, could men go back to adore the fruits, forces, and processes of nature when men no longer were animistic or pantheistic in their beliefs? To profess that the Supreme Being was especially interested in shocks of grain and shepherds at the end of the Age of Reason was to make of him a god of the garden and the ornament of a rural masque.[2]

As we shall soon see, our interest in these deistic, atheistic, and nontheistic religions is by no means an antiquarian one. It is, in fact, a consequential interest that bites deeply into the constitutional question of church-state relations. But before turning to the constitutional lessons we can learn from these and similar attempts to invent or discover religions, here is one more example of the infinite religious productivity of the human mind—an example in some ways closer to our generation than are the Religion of Reason or the Religion of the Supreme Being.

A century ago Auguste Comte projected what has been referred to as Catholicism minus Christianity. Comte was impressed with the ritual of the Catholic Church. He therefore tried to save the Catholic forms of worship and discipline but to apply them to a religion in which Humanity took the place of God. Thus parents would "baptize" their child in a ceremony in which the child would be dedicated to the service of humanity. Comte projected public observances of the Religion of Humanity, strengthened by forms of private prayer. A person was to pray four times daily, and each prayer had commemorative and purificatory parts: in the former, the worshipper would recall the name of a great benefactor of humanity, so that he might be inspired to follow his example; in the latter, he would dedicate himself to the service of humanity. Comte projected a "saints'" calendar of such great benefactors of mankind, and of course there were to be a series of festivals or sacred days. This, then, would be a religion with churches, rituals, prayers, sacraments, festivals, saints, and even a catechism. Comte's religious fervor is clear enough in many passages of his writings; the following conveys its spirit:

> The [Supreme] Being upon whom all our thoughts are concentrated is one whose existence is undoubted. We recognize that existence not in the present only, but in the past, and even in the future: and we find it always subject to one fundamental Law, by which we are enabled to conceive of it as a whole. Placing our highest happiness in universal Love, we live, as far as it is possible, for others: and this in public life as well as in private: for the two are closely linked together in our religion; a religion clothed in all the beauty of art, and yet never inconsistent with Science. After having thus exercised our powers to the full, and having given a charm and sacredness to our temporary life, we shall at last be forever incorporated into the Supreme Being, of whose life all noble natures are necessarily partakers. It is only through the worship of Humanity that we can feel the inward reality and inexpressible sweetness of this incorporation.[3]

If one were to except the details, John Stuart Mill wrote about Comte's Religion of Humanity, "there is no worthy office of a religion which this system of cultivation does not seem adequate to fulfill." [4] Indeed, elaborating on his religion, Comte argued that it made possible the convergence of feeling, reason, and action, and that at its center were the principles of Reason and Love. The religion of the Supreme Being—the religion of Humanity—thus has, Comte argued, its subjective principle, its objective dogma, and its practical object, and therefore involves "knowledge of Humanity, our affection to her love, our actions to her service." [5] From this brief résumé one can readily see the correctness of Basil Willey's judgment that Comte was a nineteenth-century Schoolman, and that his system was a Thomistic *Summa*, but one based on dogmatic science rather than on dogmatic theology.[6]

Now suppose that today a group of citizens were to form themselves into a church and profess the religion of Comte, or Robespierre, or Chaumette. Would they be entitled to claim for their religion the guaranties of the Religion Clauses of the First Amendment? These clauses do not define the term "religion." They simply provide that "Congress shall make no law respecting an establishment of religion, or prohibiting the free exercise thereof." The only other reference to religion is in Article VI, which provides that "no religious test shall ever be required as a qualification to any office or public trust under the United States." There is in the Constitution no definition of "religion" or "religious."

2

Until about the middle of this century, no American judge or court and no constitutional lawyer felt the need to concern himself with the question of definition. When a court felt called upon to test the exercise of the police power or some other power of government against the claim that its enforcement would violate the Free Exercise Clause of the First Amendment, the court then needed to speak of the things that pertained to the realm of religion; but the court could allow itself to approach the problem in conventional, popular terms.

For example, when Utah was still a Territory, Congress enacted a statute making polygamy a criminal offense. At the trial of one Reynolds for violation of the statute, the defendant established that he was a member of the Church of Jesus Christ of Latter-day Saints, commonly called the Mormon Church, which held the doctrine that it was the duty of all male members of the church to practice polygamy, and that the penalty for failure and refusal would be damnation in the life to come. Reynolds asked the trial court to instruct the jury that if he believed that his second marriage was a religious duty, the verdict must be "not guilty." The court refused so to instruct the jury. The United States Supreme Court, in 1878, upheld the conviction.[7]

The attitude of the Supreme Court is clear in the following passage from Chief Justice Waite's opinion:

> The word "religion" is not defined in the Constitution. We must go elsewhere, therefore, to ascertain its meaning, and nowhere more appropriately, we think, than to the history of the times in the midst of which the provision was adopted. The precise point of the inquiry is, what is the religious freedom which has been guaranteed?

The Court did not attempt a definition, but borrowed from statements of Madison and Jefferson language that tended to mark off jurisdictional lines between the interests and action of religion and those of government. Thus, according to Madison, " 'religion, or the duty we owe the Creator,' was not within the cognizance of civil government"; and, according to Jefferson, "it is time enough for the rightful purposes of civil government for its officers to interfere when principles break out into overt acts against peace and good order." Again according to Jefferson,

> religion is a matter which lies solely between man and his God; that he owes account to none other [than himself] for his faith or his worship; that the legislative powers of the Government reach actions only, and not opinions. . . .

Then followed Jefferson's famous metaphor of the American people "building a wall of separation between Church and State," and the expression of his hope to see "the progress of those sentiments which tend to restore man to all his natural rights, convinced he has no natural right in opposition to his social duties."

Without defining the term "religious," the Court was satisfied that whatever the word means, the First Amendment contains no prohibition against the government moving "to reach actions which were in violation of social duties or subversive of good order." The claim of religious belief, whatever "religion" might mean, would be no ground for exception from the scope of the criminal law. Laws, said the Court,

> are made for the government of actions, and while they cannot interfere with mere religious belief and opinions, they may with practices. Suppose one believed that human sacrifices were a necessary part of religious worship, would it be seriously contended that the civil government under which he lived could not interfere to prevent a sacrifice?

To permit the defendant to excuse his violation of the law because of his religious belief would be, said the Court, to make the professed doctrines of his religious belief superior to the law of the land and permit every citizen to become a law unto himself.

Today one can see some very sticky, unresolved issues in the Court's opinion in *Reynolds*. We shall consider these later, but at this point the case illustrates the judicial process by which the Court circumvented the need for a definition of "religion." The Court was satisfied with a distinction between beliefs or opinions and acts. But it failed to differentiate between acts of a religious character that are under the protection of the Free Exercise Clause and acts that are not protected. A Catholic at the Confessional or a Jew fasting on Yom Kippur is performing an *action*. In effect Reynolds claimed that his second marriage was an *acting out of his religious beliefs*, just as performing the Mass is.[8] How is one to formulate a principle by which it would be easy to distinguish polygamy—which, after all, is widely practiced among many civilized peoples and seems to have biblical approval—from other duties imposed by one's religious beliefs? We in democratic countries find insufficient the provision in the Constitution of the U.S.S.R. that limits religious liberty to "freedom of religious worship." This confines religion to what may be accomplished within the four walls of a church or synagogue; and we know how narrow, truncated, and suffocated a religion may become when it is under such strict house arrest. But the United States Supreme Court in *Reynolds* was interested in reaching a principled decision, and it needed a principle that would work in that case but not one that would necessarily also work in all future cases. As Professor Paul Freund has said, "A course of decisions may be principled without being doctrinaire." [9]

In 1890, in *Davis v. Beason*,[10] another case involving polygamy and the Mormon Church, the Supreme Court followed *Reynolds* and seemed to feel no difficulty in marking off the realm of religion and that of the state. The term "religion," said Justice Field for the Court,

> has reference to one's views of his relations to his Creator, and to the obligations they impose of reverence for his being and character, and of obedience to his will. . . . With man's relations to his Maker and the obligations he may think they impose, and the manner in which an expression shall be made by

him of his belief of those subjects, no interference can be permitted, provided always the laws of society, designed to secure its peace and prosperity, and the morals of its people are not interfered with.

What the Court said about religion seemed to be adequate for the Court's purpose in that case. It obviously was not framing a definition for a dictionary.

The pragmatic bent of the Court comes out even more clearly in a notable dissenting opinion, to which we shall want to return in the next chapter. In *United States v. Macintosh*,[11] decided in 1931, the question was whether the statutory requirements for naturalization were satisfied by an applicant who testified that he was not willing to commit himself beforehand to bear arms in defense of the United States, for he wished to reserve the right of moral judgment as to the necessity and rightness of the war. Macintosh was, in fact, what we would now call a selective conscientious objector to war. He was not opposed to all wars but only to those he considered immoral. Many young Americans now make this claim,* but in 1931 Macintosh's stand was probably unique. Of course, the issue was entirely theoretic, for in 1931 the United States was not at war; furthermore, Macintosh had been a chaplain with the Canadian Army in the First World War, and thirteen years after the Armistice he was not likely to be subject to military service. But in answer to questions, he felt compelled to say what he believed: that he could not put allegiance to country ahead of the voice of his conscience and allegiance to the will of God.

---

* The Fourth Assembly of the World Council of Churches, meeting at Uppsala, Sweden, in its statement on human rights, adopted July 16, 1968, said: "Protection of conscience demands that the churches should give spiritual care and support not only to those serving in armed forces but also to those who, especially in the light of the nature of modern warfare, object to participation in particular wars they feel bound in conscience to oppose, or who find themselves unable to bear arms or to enter the military service of their nations for reasons of conscience."

Five Justices of the Supreme Court held that Macintosh had failed to meet the requirements for naturalization; four Justices dissented. It is the dissenting opinion of Chief Justice Hughes that interests us at this juncture. "The essence of religion," said Hughes, "is belief in a relation to God involving duties superior to those arising from any human relation." At a later point in his opinion, he added: "One cannot speak of religious liberty, with proper appreciation of its essential and historic significance, without assuming the existence of a belief in supreme allegiance to the will of God." In the context presented by the facts of this case, it was sufficient for the dissenting Justices to identify religion with a belief in the necessity of obedience to a law emanating from a will superior to the will of the state.

Chief Justice Hughes probably oversimplified the issues, for there have always been those who identified the will of the state with the will of God, while there were others who saw the possibility of a conflict and urged disobedience of the law of the state if it was irreconcilable with the law of God. Thus Paul said: "Let every person be subject to the governing authorities. For there is not authority except from God, and those that exist have been instituted by God" (Rom. 13:1); but Peter said: "We must obey God rather than men" (Acts 5:29). Sometimes the same person will give contradictory counsel. In his first letter to the congregation of gentile converts in Asia Minor, Peter urges obedience to masters, respect even for harsh rulers: "Be subject for the Lord's sake to every human institution." But later in the same letter he says: "For it is better to suffer for doing right, if that should be God's will, than for doing wrong" (I Pet. 2:13; 3:17).

The ultimate issue in *Macintosh* was not, of course, to determine the will of God, but rather that of Congress. Yet the will of God did figure in the case, for both the majority and the dissenters agreed that they should assume that Congress meant to assert its will in the light of the prohibitions of the First Amendment, which includes a guarantee of the free exercise of religion. And so we are brought to the problem of the definition of "religion." The majority could have defined "religion" as including a belief in the duty to obey the governing authorities, whose existence has been instituted by God. In addition to the authority of Paul, they could have cited Jeremiah's letter to the exiles in Babylon exhorting them to establish homes and seek the welfare of the state (Jer. 29:4–9). The dissenters, as we have seen, did try to define "religion," but as including a belief in the duty to obey God rather than man.

3

But there is a serious preliminary question, and that is whether either Congress or the Court has the constitutional right to define "religion" at all. This question the Supreme Court did not face until some years later—not until 1944, in *United States v. Ballard*.[12]

Edna Ballard and Donald Ballard, organizers of the "I Am" movement, were indicted for using the mails to defraud. The indictment, in part, charged that the defendants, together with Guy W. Ballard, solicited funds and membership for the "I Am" movement by false and fraudulent representations and promises. Among the representations the indictment referred to were the following:

> that Guy W. Ballard, now deceased, alias Saint Germain, Jesus, George Washington . . . had been selected and thereby designated by the alleged "ascertained masters," Saint Germain, as a divine messenger and that . . . the words of the alleged divine entity, Saint Germain, would be transmitted to mankind through the medium of the said Guy W. Ballard.

The indictment alleged that the Ballards claimed they had been selected, by virtue of high spiritual attainments and righteous conduct, as divine messengers for the communication of the teachings of the "I Am" movement; that the Ballards claimed to have the power to heal and cure, even diseases the medical profession considered incurable, and that they had in fact cured hundreds of afflicted persons. The indictment also charged that the defendants knew that these claims were false and were made with the intention to cheat and defraud. One of the counts in the indictment was for conspiracy to defraud.

The defendants injected into the case from the very beginning the defense that their religious beliefs were being attacked and that the government sought to restrict the free exercise of their religion in violation of the First Amendment. The trial court, however, overruled motions based on this defense and restricted the issues with respect to the defendants' religious beliefs to the question of the Ballards' good faith. When the case went to the jury, the trial judge instructed it not to consider the question of the truth or falsity of the defendants' claims of supernatural powers and experiences, for example, that Jesus had appeared and dictated to them some of the works they had published. The jury was not to consider what the defendants preached, wrote, or taught. The issue put by the court to the jury was this:

> Did these defendants honestly and in good faith believe those things? If they did, they should be acquitted. . . . If these defendants did not believe those things, they did not believe that Jesus came down and dictated . . . but used the mail for the purpose of getting money, the jury should find them guilty. Therefore, gentlemen, religion cannot come into this case.

The jury found the defendants guilty. The Circuit Court of Appeals reversed the conviction and ordered a new trial. The appellate court held that the restriction of the issue to good faith was error, for the truth or falsity of the religious doctrines or beliefs of the Ballards should have been submitted to the jury.

The United States Supreme Court split three ways. Five

Justices, in an opinion by Justice Douglas, held that the trial court was right in excluding the question of the truth of the defendants' religious doctrines or beliefs. As to the issue of good faith, on the basis of which the jury found the defendants guilty, the majority side-stepped it by remanding the case to the Court of Appeals to pass on all issues other than the issue of truth of the religious beliefs.

Although it is regrettable that we do not have the Supreme Court's views on the issue of good faith, we must be grateful to have at least its views, expressed, as we shall see, in clear enough language, on the more important action to exclude from governmental concern any inquest into the truth or falsity of any person's religious beliefs or doctrines.

While freedom to act is limited, said Justice Douglas, freedom of belief is absolute. The absolute freedom of religious belief, he said,

> embraces the right to maintain theories of life and of death and of the hereafter which are rank heresy to followers of the orthodox faiths. Heresy trials are foreign to our Constitution. Men may believe what they cannot prove. They may not be put to the proof of their religious doctrines or beliefs.

Could it be supposed, asked Douglas, that an American court would be asked to pass on the truth or falsity of the miracles related in the New Testament, of "the Divinity of Christ, life after death, the power of prayer. . . ?"

> The Fathers of the Constitution were not unaware of the varied and extreme views of religious sects, of the violence of disagreements among them. . . . Man's relation to his God was made no concern of the state. He was granted the right to worship as he pleased and to answer to no man for the verity of his religious views. The religious views espoused by respondents might seem incredible, if not preposterous, to most people. But if those doctrines are subject to trial before a jury charged with finding their truth or falsity, then the same can be done with the religious beliefs of any sect.

One dare not think of the havoc that might have been caused among the American people had the Court decided against the Ballards on this constitutional issue; for then the decision could have been followed as a precedent in cases that could have been brought against other religious sects. For example, a man named George Baker started to call himself Major M. J. Divine; later he assumed the name Father Divine, and many of his followers believed him to be the personification of God. His movement has missions and "heavens" for regenerate "angels," for which Father Divine solicited and received money from tens of thousands of believers. Joseph Smith claimed that the golden tablets containing the Book of Mormon had been super-naturally revealed to him at Palmyra, New York, and the doc-trine of plural marriages was based, Brigham Young said, on a vision of Smith's. Indeed, whose religion would be exempt from criminal condemnation when tried before a jury of men and women who avowed a different religion? "Either take away religion in every case, or preserve it in every case," said Cicero some two thousand years ago. This is an anticipation of what has come to be good American constitutional doctrine. "The First Amendment does not select any one group or any one type of religion for preferred treatment," wrote Justice Douglas in *Ballard*. "It puts them all in that [preferred] posi-tion."

As we have noted, the decision in *Ballard* was five to four. One dissenting opinion was by Chief Justice Stone, in which Justices Roberts and Frankfurter joined. This opinion made two points: (1) Some counts in the indictment charged fraudulent procurement of money by knowingly making false statements as to the defendants' religious experiences. These counts, Stone argued, suffered from no constitutional infirmity. If one of the Ballards asserted that he had physically shaken hands with St. Germain in San Francisco on a certain day or that he had in fact cured hundreds of persons by the exertion of his spiritual powers, "I should not doubt," said Stone, "that it would be open to the Government to submit to the jury proof that he had never been in San Francisco and that no such cures had ever been effected." However, Stone added, there was no need in this case to pass on this issue. (2) The case went to the jury on the single issue whether the Ballards believed that the religious experiences they claimed had in fact occurred. This raised the issue of a defendant's state of mind. Now, Stone contended,

> The state of one's mind is a fact as capable of fraudulent misrepresentation as is one's physical condition or the state of his bodily health. . . . Certainly none of respondents' constitutional rights are violated if they are prosecuted for the fraudulent procurement of money by false representations as to their beliefs, religious or otherwise.

Chief Justice Stone and Justices Roberts and Frankfurter therefore concluded that the issue of belief, in good faith, in the representations of religious experiences had been properly submitted to the jury, and so the judgment of guilty should be reinstated.

The other dissenting member of the Court, Justice Jackson, said that although he was convinced that the teachings of the Ballards were "nothing but humbug," he would have dismissed the indictment and "have done with this business of judicially examining other people's faiths." He would not have allowed even the issue of good faith to reach the jury. Jackson conceded that religious leaders may be convicted of fraud for making false representations on matters other than faith or experience, for example, if they represent that funds are being used to construct a church when in fact they are being used for personal purposes. But that was not the case here. Justice Jackson made numerous interesting observations and persuasive points:

(1) What a person may believe depends on what he considers to be believable. Religious sincerity cannot, therefore, be severed from religious verity.

(2) An inquiry into intellectual honesty in religion raises the

question of religious experiences. What are these experiences? Jackson quoted the answer of William James:

> If you ask what these experiences are, they are conversations with the unseen, voices and visions, responses to prayer, changes of heart, deliverances from fear, inflowings of help, assurances of support, whenever certain persons set their own internal attitude in certain appropriate ways.

Since religious liberty includes the right to communicate such experiences to others, it seemed to Justice Jackson "an impossible task for juries to separate fancied ones from real ones, dreams from happenings, and hallucinations from true clairvoyance."

(3) What degree of skepticism or disbelief in a religious experience amounts to fraud? Jackson again quoted William James: "Faith means belief in something concerning which doubt is still theoretically possible." Belief in what one may demonstrate to the senses is not faith, said Jackson. He might have quoted the famous passage from the Epistle to the Hebrews: "Now faith is the substance of things hoped for, the evidence of things not seen" (Heb. 11:1); or the statement by Jesus to doubting Thomas: "Have you believed because you have seen me? Blessed are those who have not seen and yet believe" (John 20:29). But there are degrees of faith or belief. Even the orthodox are "sometimes accused of taking their orthodoxy with a grain of salt." Men have mental reservations as to religious symbolism. Some read the Bible literally, while others read it as allegory or metaphor. How literally is one bound to believe the doctrine he teaches, and how far does a follower rely upon the religious teacher's literal belief when he is induced to give him money?

(4) Most significant of Jackson's points is the contention that the prosecution of the Ballards was a case of misplaced emphasis. "The chief wrong which false prophets do to their following," said Jackson,

is not financial. The collections aggregate a tempting total, but individual payments are not ruinous. . . . But the real harm is on the mental and spiritual plane. . . . The wrong of these things, as I see it, is not in the money the victims part with half as much as in the mental and spiritual poison they get. But that is precisely the thing the Constitution put beyond the reach of the prosecutor, for the price of freedom of religion or of speech or of the press is that we must put up with, and even pay for, a good deal of rubbish.

Justice Jackson's telling arguments are more acceptable today than they were a quarter of a century ago; for today we see bishops of conservative, respectable denominations openly questioning fundamental Christian beliefs. What priest or minister would wish to testify under oath exactly what he believes when he uses the wafer in the Eucharist? Does he believe that the substance of the body and blood of Jesus coexist in and with the substance of the bread and wine of the Eucharist? Does he believe in the invisible miracle (transubstantiation), or does he deny transubstantiation yet affirm the real presence of Jesus? How present is the real presence? To Jackson—and, one suspects, to the five Justices who composed the majority—the Ballards could not be prosecuted without opening the door to the possibility of general religious persecution. Neither the truth or falsity of religious beliefs, nor the good or bad faith with which they are held or taught, can become legal issues where religious liberty is guaranteed. "The heart," Jeremiah said, "is deceitful above all things, and desperately wicked" (Jer. 17:9); and the Psalmist taught that the heart is deep and that God alone knows its secrets (Pss. 21:8; 64:6).

It speaks well for the American record of religious liberty that although the early Mormons were persecuted by other Christians, the government did not attempt to prosecute them for crimes other than polygamy; and the spirit of religious liberty has effectively shielded countless churches and sects that have made the wildest imaginable claims in the name of their religions. Today Mormons are quite respectable. Leaders of their church have been members of the Cabinet, and one of them, the Governor of Michigan, was an aspirant for the Republican nomination for President. No one sought to disqualify him because of his religion.* Two Unitarians—Fillmore and Taft—have been President of the United States; Hoover was a Quaker; and the religious views of Jefferson, John Adams, John Quincy Adams, and Abraham Lincoln were unorthodox. It is relevant to mention that in 1964 more than twenty-seven million Americans voted for Barry Goldwater, knowing that his father was born a Jew—and that Goldwater's support was among the conservative elements of the American people.

4

In 1966 two cases in which aspects of the *Ballard* case became relevant came before American courts. One involved the tax-exemption status of the Foundation for Divine Meditation, of which Merle E. Parker was the founder and director.[13] Parker had a degree from an institution that called itself the College of Universal Truth. His Foundation for Divine Meditation acquired a building in Valley Center, California, where he conducted religious services. The Foundation also sponsored swimming and skating parties on its property. Parker wrote and published many tracts, which he promoted and sold by mail. He published a newspaper, *The National Christian Crusader*, which promoted his publications. He also published and sold courses pertaining to metaphysics, philosophy, faith healing, physical and psychological self-development, and diets. Some publications had as their objective the promise of financial

* Scientology as a religion has come into conflict with the law for labeling a skin galvanometer. The federal Court of Appeals held that since the literature concerns religious doctrine, it cannot, under *Ballard*, be deemed labeling. *Founding Church of Scientology v. United States*, 37 LW 2466 (1969).

rewards. One project, for example, was the stimulation of membership in the Santa Ysabel Ming Tree Society. Upon payment of dues, the member would receive ming tree seeds with instructions, which, if followed, promised one thousand dollars' worth of trees growing on a single window sill. There was also Parker's "$25,000 Pyramid Plan," which taught the purchaser how to raise earthworms for profit. A ten-lesson plan, costing $23.30, promised earnings of $1000 within six months. There was a "Christian Healing Crusade," which requested donations for prayers. Parker and his Foundation for Divine Meditation were a thriving business; in one year the gross income was $207,000, in another, $290,000.

In the light of these and related facts, the United States Court of Appeals held that the evidence clearly supported the finding of the Tax Court that the foundation was pursuing a substantial nonexempt purpose. But we should carefully note that the Court of Appeals was careful to place its decision on the configuration of the peculiar factual situations it found in the evidence. The decision was principled but not doctrinaire. "We are not saying," the court wrote,

> that religious organizations may not maintain their tax-exempt status if they conduct healing crusades, take stands for or against moral issues, publish newsletters, or offer their literature for sale. The non-religious purpose of this particular organization was evidenced by the extent and scope of the profit-making circulation, the methods of promotion, the general non-religious subject-matter of some of the publications, the large annual profit, the substantial accumulated earnings, and the statements made by Dr. Parker. When all of this is viewed in relationship to the organization's exempt activities, the substantial nature of the non-religious purpose is established.

Earlier in its opinion the court said: "There can be no doubt that the [worship] services and the sponsored recreational activities [swimming and skating parties] were religious in nature and had [the foundation] so restricted its activities, its exempt status would probably not be questioned."

This decision of the Court of Appeals, though not one to arouse strong feelings, reminds one of the Supreme Court's unfortunate decision in *Ginzburg v. United States.*[14] There the Court did not decide that the publications, standing alone, would be considered obscene, but held that the publications, "against a background of commercial exploitation of erotica solely for the sake of their prurient appeal," were obscene. The Court of Appeals considered Parker's activities in the same way. It was the commercial success of Parker that was his undoing. Suppose he had engaged in the same activities but with less nerve, with less of the Madison Avenue techniques, with more feigned diffidence, and with much less financial success, would his activities then have been commercial rather than religious in character? Clergymen of almost all denominations bless personal, commercial, national, military, and political ventures, and in one way or another grant indulgences that mitigate the punishment of sins, and pray for the comfort of persons who are assumed to be living in another world—often for a donation to themselves or their churches.

Our legislatures and courts have not shown much zeal for the protection of the helpless consumer. Only now are we beginning to hear of a need for laws to assure a measure of truth in advertising and in the packaging of wares. For example, the law did little to help the buyer of an automobile in claims against the manufacturer.[15] The general rule still is expressed in the maxim *caveat emptor:* let the buyer examine, judge, test, and decide for himself—let him take all the risks. If this rule obtains in what are patently commercial business transactions, which are not under the protection of the First Amendment, should it not apply a fortiori to the numerous activities of churches in which they put out their hand for a contribution? As Chief Judge of the New York Court of Appeals, Cardozo declared that one who is a trustee owes "the duty of the finest loyalty. . . . A trustee is held to something stricter than the morals of the market place. Not honesty alone, but the punctilio of an honor the most sensitive, is then the standard of behavior." [16] But this high standard of morality has by no means been demanded in the business world generally, and it would, one fears, lead to endless bitter conflict if the standard formulated by Cardozo were to be applied to churches, synagogues, religious organizations, and clergymen. It would mean the erosion of the Free Exercise Clause of the First Amendment.

The second case worth mention involved a will contest in a California court.[17] David Supple's will left a substantial portion of his estate to various Roman Catholic charities. A grand-nephew attacked the will on the ground that the will had been obtained by fraud and undue influence. The lower court admitted the will to probate. On appeal, the court summarized the allegations in the following terms—the charges against the Roman Catholic Church were so unusual that it is best to give them in the court's own words. It was alleged

> that the testator had been a devout Roman Catholic from his earliest childhood until the time of his death. . . . Allegedly the testator was taught that every human being has an immortal soul which can experience both pleasure and pain and which, upon the death of the body, is consigned either to Heaven, Hell or Purgatory; that Heaven is a place of complete and eternal bliss, Hell is a place of complete and eternal torment, and Purgatory is a place of temporary torment; that the consignment of a person's soul to one of these three regions is dependent upon the degree to which the person complied during his lifetime, with certain rules and commands which were prescribed by God but as to which the Roman Catholic Church, God's Vicar and representative on earth, has been appointed the depositary, interpreter and promulgator; that the soul of a person who dies while wilfully guilty of violating any important rule will be consigned to Hell and the soul of a person guilty of lesser derelictions will be consigned to Purgatory until his offenses shall have been ex-

piated; that in order for a person's soul to enter Heaven, he must have faith and must also have performed certain good works, which may include the bestowal of gifts, legacies and devises upon the Church and its divisions or agents; that as a reward for such good works, the priests and agents of the Church will recite prayers and perform ceremonials which will have the effect of facilitating the consignment of his soul to Heaven or shortening the period within which his soul, or that of another person whom he may designate, shall be required to spend in Purgatory. It was further alleged that the testator firmly believed all of the above representations and executed his will in reliance upon them and in the belief that the salvation of his soul and the souls of his predeceased relatives might be procured if he left the bulk of his estate to the Church and its agents, agencies and divisions. It was also alleged that all of the above representations were in fact false and untrue, constituting childish superstitions incompatible with man's advanced position in science and technology, and that the charitable beneficiaries who made these representations were guilty of unduly influencing the testator and were also guilty of fraud because they had made positive assertions which, although they believed them to be true, were not warranted by the information which they had and because they had breached a duty which, without an actually fraudulent intent, gained them an advantage by misleading the testator to his prejudice and the prejudice of his heirs at law.

The California Court of Appeals, affirming the judgment, followed the majority of the *Ballard* case by holding that the court would not go into the truth or falsity of religious beliefs. It pointed out, moreover, that there was no allegation that the Roman Catholic churchmen did not in fact believe the teachings attributed to them—that there was no allegation of lack of honesty or good faith. Had these allegations been made, apparently the Roman Catholic Church would have been put to the proof that the Church in fact honestly, sincerely maintains the beliefs attributed to it by David Supple's grandnephew. I cannot conceive of a stronger support of Justice Jackson's position in *Ballard* than the possibility of an American court listening to and passing on evidence as to such questions. Such a case would easily open the door to what would be equivalent to witch hunts and heresy trials.

5

The word "religion" was placed in the First Amendment not to stir up strife but to avoid it. This is the social justification of the Free Exercise Clause. It is not that Madison and Jefferson and the other leaders of American thought in 1791 put a premium on the superstitions, deceptions, hypocrisies, and perversions that often were cloaked in religious garb. The Free Exercise Clause was not written with the intention to protect imbecility and mendacity, no more than that the guarantee against self-incrimination in the Fifth Amendment was put in for the protection of criminals. But just as there is no protection of the innocent unless the guilty are also protected, so there is no protection of the truth and of sincerity unless the false and the dishonest are also protected. In the *New York Times* libel case* the Supreme Court pointed out that for debate to be free, there must be freedom for erroneous statement if there is to be room for the truth; for if a man will be allowed to speak only the truth he will be safe only when he is silent. Freedom of speech, therefore, needs "breathing space" for speech that is not truthful. The Court, of course, recognized that this principle leaves the door open to excesses and abuses, but this possibility does not weaken or limit the constitutional guarantee. Especially is this so with religious faith, where "the tenets of one man may seem the rankest error to his neighbor." [18] But unless a society considers truth and honesty as the prime values, overshadowing

---

* *New York Times Co. v. Sullivan*, 376 U.S. 254 (1964). The decision in this case is comparable to the decision in *Ballard*, and concurring opinions of Black and Goldberg are comparable to the opinion of Jackson in *Ballard*.

all others, "breathing space" must be left for error and dishonesty. As long as there is constitutional protection of the free exercise of religion—and of speech and press—and as long as these freedoms are even given a preferred position,[19] there can be no test of "the truth, popularity, or social utility of the ideas and beliefs which are offered." [20] That there have been and will be gross abuses, no one can doubt. But this possibility was foreseen from the very foundation of constitutional government in the United States. "Some degree of abuse," said Madison, "is inseparable from the proper use of everything; and in no instance is this more true than in that of the press." [21] Were Madison alive today and were he to observe the bewilderingly complex religious scene in the United States, he would say that in no instance is this more true than in that of religion.

But not only should the questions of religious truth or falsity and of sincerity or hypocrisy of religious professions be beyond the cognizance of government, but even the very meaning or definition of "religion," as the term is used in the First Amendment, should be outside the area of governmental inquiry.[22] But this proposition needs further exploration, which it will receive in the next chapter.

3. Religion and Secularism

1

We have considered several of the more baffling aspects of the scope of the Free Exercise Clause of the First Amendment, and our thinking led us to conclude that the truth or falsity of religious beliefs or claims—regardless how intellectually, morally, or aesthetically outrageous they may seem—is beyond the cognizance of the law. We also concluded, with Justice Jackson, that the question of sincerity or hypocrisy, the question of honesty, also should be beyond the reach of the law. Of these two propositions, the former is by far the more important, for it affects the whole of a religion and all its adherents. If the law could brand some religions as false and deprive them of the protection of the First Amendment, the law might thereby violate the Establishment Clause as well as the Free Exercise Clause, for it would favor some religions and penalize others. The Establishment Clause, the Supreme Court unanimously agreed,

> means at least this: Neither a state nor the Federal Government can set up a church. Neither can pass laws which aid one religion, aid all religions, or prefer one religion over another.[1]

For a court to find that certain professed religious beliefs are true or false—that Moses received the Torah from God at Sinai; or that Jesus, after three days in the tomb, rose from the dead; or that Mohammed had a vision in the cave of Mt. Hira, and that thereafter and throughout his life he continued to have revelations; or that the golden tablets containing the Book of Mormon were revealed to Joseph Smith at Palmyra, New York; or that Father Divine is God; or that Guy Ballard had shaken hands and talked with Jesus—is to have the power to prefer one religion over another. By closing up one church, the state aids the churches it permits to remain open. Thus, as we see, the implications of the *Ballard* case are indeed far-reaching.

But an even more difficult and more important question remains: What is "religion"? This question is, of course, closely related to the question of the truth or falsity of religious beliefs, but the questions are not identical. The question of truth is a question for logic, or science, or experience; while the other question is one of definition. If, for example, nontheistic beliefs —like those of Comte—do not constitute a "religion," then such beliefs can make no claims, even if they are true, under the Religion Clauses of the First Amendment.

One way to approach the question of defining "religion," as the term is used in the Constitution, is to ask what the word meant to the advocates of the Bill of Rights, especially Thomas Jefferson. We know that Jefferson went to France in 1785 when he succeeded Benjamin Franklin as minister, and he was there in 1789, at the beginning of the Revolution, which had his sympathetic interest. He no doubt knew the extreme views on religion that were then current among French intellectuals. It was in 1789 too that Madison, responding to the urgent pleas of Jefferson, introduced in the first session of Congress what came to be the Bill of Rights. Jefferson's position can be briefly stated: The government has absolutely no power over a man's *beliefs*. The power of the state may be directed only as to *actions*. It is, said Jefferson,

> time enough for the rightful purposes of civil government, for its officers to interfere when principles break out into overt acts against peace and good order.[2]

In his *Notes on Virginia* (1801), Jefferson argued that government has authority only over such "natural rights as we have submitted to them" and

> the rights of conscience we never submitted, we could not submit. We are answerable for them to our God. The legitimate powers of government extend to such acts only as are injurious to others. But it does me no injury for my neighbor to say there are twenty Gods or no God. It neither picks my pocket nor breaks my leg.[3]

In the following year, in his famous letter to the Danbury Baptist Association, in which he spoke of the "wall of separation between Church and State," Jefferson wrote "that the legislative powers of the Government reach actions only, and not opinions."

From the standpoint of this overt-act approach, to which Jefferson consistently adhered with regard to religious liberty,[4] the state may not define "religion." "To define is to limit," said Chief Justice Hughes;[5] and any limitation on the constitutional meaning of "religion" might exclude beliefs maintained by some as their religion. As any reader of the Bible or of the literature of ancient Greece and Rome knows, history has been a prolific producer of religions, from the most vile, brutal, and obscene, to the most refined, gentle, and beautiful. Surely the framers of the Bill of Rights knew this very well. And in this respect history continues to be a dynamic force: old religions are changing in significant ways, and new religions are constantly being created. They must all be accommodated by the First Amendment, and this can be accomplished only if it is not used as a Procrustean bed.

2

The United States in particular has seen—since the ratification of the Bill of Rights in 1791—the creation of many new sects and religions. There can be little doubt that the two clauses of the First Amendment have greatly contributed to the prodigality of the religious spirit among the American people. Indeed, it is doubtful that anywhere else in the Western world, at any time in history, have so many religions been spawned and have existed side by side—hundreds and hundreds of denominations and sects. *The Yearbook of American Churches for 1968*, published by the National Council of Churches, lists 241 religious bodies reporting. There are many others for which there are no statistics. Many of them—like political parties—came into existence by the process of splintering or fission. But no matter what their paternity may be, constitutionally all are legitimate. As far back as 1872 the Supreme Court ruled that "the law [of the United States] knows no heresy. . . ." [6] This is a constitutional way of saying, in effect, that the Constitution knows no definition of "religion."

In recent years American courts have felt themselves compelled to describe, if not technically to define, "religion" in the broadest terms. In a California case the question was whether the building of the Fellowship of Humanity was entitled to tax exemption as a property used for religious worship. The court found from the evidence that the humanists have no place in their beliefs for a divine or superhuman being or for a Supreme Being. But the court took a purely practical or pragmatic view of the matter. It held that a building is used for religious worship if the things that are done there are pretty much the same sort of things that one would find if one looked into a building that was concededly a church. That is to say, if it "makes like" a church, it is a church. The court found that the humanists met on Sunday mornings, and the program or order of service included some moments of silent meditation; the singing of some "Fellowship Songs for the New Era"; a public reading from a newspaper or magazine or, occasionally, from the Bible; and a talk on a subject of interest to humanists, followed by a period of questions and answers. The session closed with a collection and another few moments of silent meditation. There were no audible prayers. The court held that where the activities of a group were similar to those of theistic religious groups, except for lack of belief in a Supreme Being, the property was entitled to tax exemption on the ground that it was used for religious worship.[7]

At the same time, the United States Court of Appeals had before it a similar case involving the Washington Ethical Society.[8] This group was part of the Ethical Culture Movement, which has about thirty local societies in the United States. The movement was founded in 1876 by Felix Adler, who left the rabbinate and Judaism when he came under the influence of Kant and of the neo-Kantian German philosopher Friedrich Albert Lange. He founded a new group based on three objectives:

> sex purity, the principle of devoting the surplus of one's income beyond that required for one's genuine needs to the elevation of the working class, and, finally, continued intellectual development.

Adler thought that his society would "take the place of the consecrating influence of the old religions." The society meets for Sunday services, where there is no prayer and no ritual, but only music, readings, and an address. Members are committed to no creed. Their approach to life and the world is a naturalistic one, based on scientific knowledge and scientific methods. The society conducts forums, classes, clubs, and a summer camp. It has no ministers but rather officials called "leaders," who have been authorized by public officials to perform marriage ceremonies—not as judges or mayors or ship captains are, but like priests, ministers, or rabbis, because their group is recognized as a "religious society."

The Court of Appeals concluded that the society qualified for tax exemption as a church or a religious society. The court held that a belief in a Supreme Being or a supernatural power was not essential to qualify for tax exemption on religious grounds. Indeed, the court said, to limit the exemption to orthodox religious groups would raise constitutional issues under the Establishment Clause.

Both these cases were decided in 1957. Four years later the United States Supreme Court took advantage of an opportunity to make a notable contribution toward resolving this issue.

Roy Torcaso was appointed a notary public in Maryland, but he was then refused a commission to serve because he would not declare his belief in God. The Declaration of Rights of the Maryland Constitution provided that no religious test shall be required as a qualification for any state office "other than a declaration of belief in the existence of God." The Supreme Court unanimously held that the Maryland requirement was unconstitutional.[9]

In his opinion for the Court, Justice Black said that no government in the United States can force or influence a person to go to or stay away from a church, or force him to profess a belief or disbelief in any religion; that no person can be punished for entertaining or professing religious beliefs or disbeliefs; that neither a state nor the Federal Government

> can constitutionally pass laws or impose requirements which aid all religions as against non-believers, and neither can aid those religions based on a belief in the existence of God as against those religions founded on different beliefs.

The Court at this point added the following significant footnote:

> Among religions in this country which do not teach what would generally be considered a belief in the existence of God are Buddhism, Taoism, Ethical Culture, Secular Humanism and others.

And the Court cited for this proposition in the footnote the two cases from California and the Court of Appeals that we have already discussed. It concluded that Maryland's religious test for public office unconstitutionally invaded Torcaso's "freedom of belief and religion," and therefore could not be enforced against him.

The Court has been criticized for giving such wide latitude to the term "religion" in its constitutional setting as to embrace Secular Humanism, Ethical Culture, and the faith of the atheist. But one may say that the Court had no alternative in view of the great latitude ordinarily given to the term "religion" in current religious and even popular thought. The Court could not begin to limit by definition the reach of the term without finding itself in the most dangerous mire.

Indeed, even the term "atheism" cannot be defined without an essay on the history of its usage. The Romans called Jews and Christians atheists because they would not pay the customary honors to the imperial cult. The ancient rabbis called atheists "Epicureans" because the latter denied that the gods interfered in human affairs. Plato called atheists those who believed that gods could be influenced by sacrifice or flattery to interfere in human affairs. The rabbis of the Talmud called Adam the first atheist because, by hiding from God, he denied God's omnipresence. To some, anthropomorphic beliefs are atheistic; to others, the denial of a providential rule of the universe by a being with exaggerated human traits is atheistic.

In its *Pastoral Constitution on the Church in the Modern World* (1965), Vatican Council II deals with the fact that the word "atheism" is applied to diverse phenomena. Some atheists, the document says, expressly deny God; other atheists hold only that man can assert absolutely nothing about Him. Many atheists use "such a method so to scrutinize the question of God"—apparently referring here to language analysis—"as to make it seem devoid of meaning." Then there are those who insist that the scientific method can explain everything. Some laud man so extravagantly that they seem more inclined to affirm man than to deny God. Others put up a false idea of God and then reject that idea, but in fact they do not reject the

God of the Bible. Some men, says the document, simply have no religious experience, and so see no reason why they should trouble themselves about religion. Still others are atheists simply because they mean to protest violently against the evil in the world. The document suggests, too, that some men become atheists as a critical reaction against religious beliefs, and even against Christianity in particular; and for atheism due to this cause, believers—by teaching erroneous doctrines, by living lives deficient in religious, moral, or social values—share responsibility.[10]

These and other observations on atheism in this document demonstrate the difficulty of defining the term. A hairline often separates the theist from the atheist; the same man may be both at the same time, or either one or the other on successive days or moments. The presence in the scriptural canon of Ecclesiastes, a book bristling with ideas that suggest skepticism and heresy, graphically shows how the religious mind itself is ambivalent on the most fundamental issues; no less revealing in this way is the Book of Job, with its shattering views of death, sin, evil, and suffering. We must remember that Job is vindicated and that Job's friends, with their glib pieties about the providential governance of the world, are repudiated by the Lord.

The problem of a definition of "atheism," as we see, is so closely linked with a definition of "religion" that for the Supreme Court to attempt to define either term would make of the Court an ecclesiastical tribunal sitting to decide issues of orthodoxy and heresy.

3

In the cases that involved humanists and the Ethical Culture Society, the courts did not really attempt definitions of "religion." As we said, they took a practical line, one that sufficed for their purposes. The courts did not pretend that they had found an absolute answer, but only that their answers would suffice, that they would be good enough to live by. The essence of these decisions can be stated in two propositions, one substantive and the other methodological.

The substantive proposition is that the Establishment Clause requires the conclusion that the word "religion" in the First Amendment encompasses religions that do not worship a Supreme Being or a supernatural power as well as those that do. The courts have not pushed the substantive inquiry beyond the necessities of the cases before them.

The methodological proposition is that the court will hear evidence as to what people do when they assemble in a building that they claim to be a place of religious worship. If they act as people generally do at a religious service, then they are engaged in an act of worship. This is a common-sense approach to a sticky question, and it sufficed for the two cases.

But one can readily see that this rough-and-tumble approach may be too restrictive when the group acts in uncommon ways. Here are several recent examples.

Zoning ordinances may restrict certain areas to residential purposes. Suppose a congregation wants to build a church or synagogue in such an area. Most courts have held that churches and synagogues may not be barred from residential districts. They have held that to exclude them from a residential district will not further the purpose of zoning, which is the promotion of the health, safety, and moral or general welfare of the community. Furthermore, to compel churches to build only in industrial or business districts might be an impairment of the free exercise of religion. We are not questioning here the rightness of these decisions (though it should be stated that the courts of California and Wisconsin have decided against churches and the Supreme Court has dismissed appeals).[11]

Now, some orthodox Jewish students at Princeton University —members of the Yavneh organization—purchased a house in an area restricted to private residential purposes. They lived in the house, maintained a kosher kitchen, conducted study groups, and held religious services three times a day and on the Sabbath and holidays. Neighbors filed objections with the town's zoning board, alleging that the group was maintaining the house in violation of the zoning ordinance. The board at first upheld the neighbors; then at a rehearing the board heard the testimony of rabbis that in Judaism a synagogue is not limited to worship in the sense of prayer. They in effect argued that the methodological approach used by the courts in the cases of the humanists and the Ethical Culture Society will not work in the case of Judaism. A synagogue, they showed from traditional Jewish sources, may also feel compelled to feed the hungry who will avoid nonkosher food, and to provide shelter, in a congenial Jewish environment, for the wayfarer. The house was, they said, used as a "synagogue," provided it is understood that the term be given a traditional Jewish meaning and not the conventional non-Jewish meaning of "church." The zoning board accepted this argument and ruled in favor of the Jewish student group.

This is not the occasion to argue for or against this decision, but the case is useful as an illustration of the dangers involved in relying exclusively on a single approach in cases involving religion.

There are several other cases that point up this problem.

One will not find the Native American Church in the statistical report of the *Yearbook of American Churches*, yet it has a membership of 200,000,[12] with branches in seventeen states. In recent years it has attracted public attention by its brushes with the law. Apparently the Native American Church had its origin in Mexico, and has spread among the Indians in our West. The religious ceremonial of its adherents focuses on the use of "buttons" of the dried peyote plant. In this peyote ceremonial the participants—up to thirty or forty in number—squat in a room from sundown Saturday to dawn Sunday. They chant, blow bird whistles, pass "prayer cigarettes" rolled on the scene with Bull Durham tobacco, and chew the peyote, four "buttons" at a time (four is considered a magic number). The peyote induces visions, which inspire individual singing and occasional confessional monologues and prayers, in which the plant is spoken of reverently along with the Holy Trinity of Christianity. The beliefs are half pagan and half Christian.[13]

California was one of the few states that prohibited the use of peyote. In April 1962 three Navahos were arrested as they participated among thirty members in a peyote service in a hogan built of railroad ties. A California Superior Court judge, after a two-day trial, found the defendants guilty.[14] In 1964, in *People v. Woody*,[15] the California Supreme Court reversed the convictions. The court found that the use of peyote plays a central theological role for members of the Native American Church. The drug, which induces a state of hallucination, is used as a sacrament. Those who use it ceremonially claim that it acts as a "teacher" because it induces a feeling of brotherhood with other persons and enables the user to experience God. Members of the church consider the nonreligious use of peyote sacrilegious. Indeed, said the court, peyote is in a way even more than a sacrament, since prayers are directed to it as prayers are directed to the Deity or the Holy Spirit. The court found the ban on peyote to be a violation of religious liberty.

But this is not the focus of our present interest. The case is cited here only to point out that the methodological approach, which may be warranted in cases involving a humanist or an Ethical Culture service, may not be useful in an offbeat situation like that presented by the Native American Church, whose ritual, to most people, would recall a session of hippies rather than a church or synagogue worship service. Had the California case involved the question of tax exemption of property of the

Native American Church used as a place of religious worship, the approach used in the other cases would have been useless. Just as the First Amendment stands in the way of a definition of "religion," so, too, does it stand in the way of any attempt to make absolute the meaning of "worship" or "prayer." The maximum latitude and fluidity are required by both the Establishment and the Free Exercise Clauses.*

4

It is not difficult to foresee troublesome cases involving such issues. Consider, for example, the problem of Timothy Leary, who on September 19, 1966, proclaimed that he had founded a new religion, the League of Spiritual Discovery (L.S.D.). Leary had a Ph.D. degree in clinical psychology. He wrote extensively on the use of psychedelic drugs in the treatment of mental illness. He founded the Kaiser Psychiatric Clinic at Oakland, California, and received substantial grants from the Federal Government for his research work. He published diagnostic tests for mental illness that have been used extensively in diagnosing and treating mental illness and have been translated into foreign languages. Before starting to teach at Harvard in 1959, he had taught for several years at the University of California as a member of its medical faculty. He was dismissed from the Harvard University faculty in 1963 for his use of students in LSD (lysergic acid diethylamide) experiments.

In 1960 Leary visited Mexico. He later testified that during this visit he had "the most intense religious experience" he had ever had in his life, as the result of having eaten some of the "sacred mushrooms" of Mexico. The incident changed his life. Between then and 1966 he wrote five books and thirty-eight articles on the religious and scientific use of psychedelic drugs, and since the incident with the "sacred mushrooms" he has de-

* See page ix.

voted his life to attempting to understand the religious experience and how it can be used to help others. He formed a religious research group at Harvard, and, with the help of Aldous Huxley, experimented with certain psychedelic drugs. In 1962 he studied Hinduism, and after a year's study became a member of a Hindu sect. After his dismissal from Harvard, he pursued his experimental work in Mexico, and then established a center and workshop for religious and scientific research at Millbrook, New York. He used the building also as a place for religious meditation and as a spiritual retreat. Rooms in the house contained shrines devoted to Hindu, Buddhist, and Christian ways of finding God, and there were religious pictures and statues. He traveled in Asia in furtherance of his religious search and studied Buddhism and Hinduism with monks and religious teachers. While studying in India with Sri Asoke Fukir, a religious leader, Leary participated in religious rituals in which marihuana was used. When he became a Hindu, he joined, in Massachusetts, the Brahmakrishna sect.

Leary first used marihuana in 1964. It enabled him, he said, to attain what he called the third level of consciousness. Other psychedelic drugs, he said, take a person to a higher level. In Hinduism there are thousands of roads to illumination, to reach the god within the person, and different sects specialize in different aids to achieve this. The Brahmakrishna sect uses marihuana for religious illumination and meditation. He has said that he uses marihuana less than once a week, and then only for religious purposes. Leary said he makes no distinction between his religious beliefs and his scientific experimentation.

Now we come to Leary's involvements with the criminal law. In December 1965 Leary, accompanied by his two children and two other persons, left New York by automobile for the Yucatan, in Mexico, for a Christmas vacation and in order to work on a book and prepare for a summer session with a research group at Millbrook. At the Laredo International Bridge, in Texas, customs officials found marihuana in the car and on the person of Leary's daughter. Leary claimed the marihuana was his and told the officials that he had obtained it in New York.

At his trial in March 1966 Leary testified that he used the drug for religious and scientific purposes and contended that it would be a violation of his religious beliefs and practices if he were denied its use. There was supporting testimony that the Brahmakrishna sect is recognized throughout India by all Hindus, that marihuana plays a very important part in the rituals of the Hindu sect conducted by Sri Asoke Fukir in India, and that the effect of marihuana and other psychedelic drugs is to expand consciousness and to heighten intellectual activity and sensory awareness.

After a trial before a jury, the Federal District Court found Leary guilty, and he was sentenced to imprisonment for thirty years and a fine of $30,000. His conviction was unanimously upheld by the United States Court of Appeals on September 29, 1967.[16]

Six months after his conviction, and a year before the appellate court handed down its judgment, Leary announced that he had founded a new religion based on the sacramental use of LSD, marihuana, and peyote. His League of Spiritual Discovery, he said, "like every great religion of the past," would seek to find "the divinity within and to express this revelation in a life of glorification and worship of God." He added that he would redefine the ancient goals in "the metaphor of the present—turn on, tune in, and drop out." He said that the sect already had 411 members, and that he expected more than a million persons to join within the next two or three years.

Members of the sect, according to Leary, would need to list with the League which rooms in their homes would be designated as "religious shrines" where the drugs would be taken at stated times—LSD once every seven days (it is ineffective more often) and marihuana one hour a day. These drugs and peyote would be the "sacramental substance" of the new religion. Leary explained his six-word motto as follows:

> Turn on means to go beyond your secular tribal mind to contact the many levels of divine energy which lie within your consciousness; tune in means to express and to communicate your new revelations in visible acts of glorification, gratitude and beauty; drop out means to detach yourself harmoniously, tenderly and gracefully from worldly commitments until your entire life is dedicated to worship and search.[17]

Before we turn to a consideration of some of the constitutional questions involved, we should note that as bizarre as the new sect may appear at first blush, it in fact has respectable precedents in the United States.

A man who comes readily to mind in this connection is William James. In a letter about his Gifford Lectures, *Varieties of Religious Experience* (1902), James wrote:

> The mother sea and fountain-head of all religions lie in the mystical experiences of the individual, taking the word mystical in a very wide sense. All theologies and all ecclesiasticisms are secondary growths superimposed. . . . I attach the mystical or religious consciousness to the possession of an extended subliminal self, with a thin partition through which messages make irruption. We are thus made convincingly aware of the presence of a sphere of life larger and more powerful than our usual consciousness, with which the latter is nevertheless continuous. The impressions and impulsions and emotions and excitements which we thence receive help us to live, they found [lay the foundation for] invincible assurance of a world beyond sense, they melt our hearts and communicate significance and value to everything and make us happy.[18]

Students of James have pointed out that his Gifford Lectures defended *variety*; that James did not attempt to define religion but spoke of "the life of religion"; that the examples he cited "ranged all the way from mild intuition to hearing voices and seeing visions emanating from the spirit world." [19] James thought that there were different ways by which men try to expand their consciousness by opening windows or peepholes into the subliminal—or transliminal—world. Our lives, he wrote,

> are like islands in the sea, or like trees in the forest . . . [which] commingle their roots in the darkness underground, and the islands also hang together through the ocean's bottom. Just so there is a continuum of cosmic consciousness, against which our individuality builds but accidental fences, and into which our several minds plunge as into a mother-sea or reservoir.[20]

Just as Pope John XXIII sought *aggiornamento* for the Catholic Church by opening a window upon the outside world, so, James would say, a person seeks a "window" into the unseen world, the unknown, the perception of which may require a paranormal sensitivity.[21] It was natural for James, therefore, to engage in and encourage others in all kinds of research into religious experiences—research into faith healing, psychical phenomena, telepathy, and survival after death—and he constantly insisted on the legitimacy and importance of such inquiries. One can suppose that James would have agreed with Leary that there is no solid line between religious experience and scientific investigation in this area and, furthermore, that experimentation with psychedelic drugs may be as warranted as experimentation with spiritualism or the Mass or prayer with phylacteries.

Recently the poet Allen Ginsberg, who is a member of the Shiva sect of Hinduism, has written that when he was twenty-eight years of age, he had a series of "visionary or religious or illuminative experiences," in which he had an auditory hallucination of William Blake's voice and

> also experienced a number of moments of guilelessness about the world around me and feeling that the father of the universe had existed all along but I had not realized it, that the father of the universe loved me and that I was identical with the father. So this was an experience of bliss. I realized that I had my place in the universe.

Ginsberg wrote that the common quality in psychedelic experiences is "that there is a break in the normal mode of consciousness, an opening up of another universe of awareness." All who have had these experiences, he says, cry out in delight that

> the universe they had taken for granted had suddenly opened and revealed itself as something much deeper and fuller, much more exquisite, something more connected with a divine sense of things—a Self perhaps . . . the non-conditioned, non-verbal, non-conceptual opening up of the mind to all of the data of experience flooding in at once, newly perceived, or perceived as a newborn babe or early child.[22]

One cites these examples of the central role of psychedelic drugs in religious experience—in the lives of some persons— not of course to recommend their use, but to underscore the conclusion that the case of Leary's League of Spiritual Discovery raises some serious constitutional issues. I would say that Leary's sect is entitled to full protection of the Free Exercise Clause.* *How* a vision or any other religious experience is induced or vouchsafed has nothing to do with the fact that the person has had it. Perhaps the experience of Elijah the prophet in the cave on Mount Horeb came to him after taking a psychedelic drug?

> And behold, the Lord passed by, and a great and strong wind rent the mountains, and broke in pieces the rocks before the Lord; but the Lord was not in the wind; and after the wind an earthquake; but the Lord was not in the earthquake; and after the earthquake a fire; but the Lord was not in the fire; and after the fire a still small voice [or a sound of thin silence] (I Kings 19: 11–12, Soncino ed., p. 139).

The same question is suggested, too, by the experience of Paul. He relates that he had been commissioned to go to Damascus

---

* This does not, however, necessarily mean that Leary was exempt from the federal narcotics law. This question will be considered in the next chapter.

to help suppress Christianity there. As he approached the city, he suddenly saw a blinding light and heard Jesus ask, "Why persecutest thou me?" Paul was temporarily blinded and had to be led into the city. The experience converted him (Acts 9:1–19; 22:3–21; 26:9–23). He spent part of the next thirteen years in the Arabian desert before he set out on his first missionary journey. Or we could consider in this context the experience of Joseph Smith when the Book of Mormon was revealed to him at Palmyra, or the vision of Joseph Smith that came to Brigham Young. Are these experiences, in their substance and apart from their cause, essentially different from Allen Ginsberg's hearing the voice and words of William Blake?

5

If the Constitution is not interested in the question of the truth or falsehood of religious professions, confessions, or revelations, then we must put them all on an equal footing, and protect them all without partiality. The clearest and surest way to this end is for the government not to inquire into the truth of religious claims or the degree of sincerity with which they are maintained.

In refusing to examine into the truth of religious claims, our courts but follow the common-sense dictates of mankind; for almost by instinct every man knows that he cannot, a man's life being what it is, go out to seek for and find the one true religion. The fifteenth-century Jewish philosopher Joseph Albo makes an interesting argument for this point, for a purpose, of course, other than our own.

Suppose, said Albo, a man sets out to investigate the principles of his religion to see whether they are true. The process would necessitate his examining another religion as well as his own. In the first place, the very undertaking would imply that he has doubts about the truth of his own religion, and this means that he forfeits a reward for belief that is firm and free from doubt. In any case, suppose his investigation leads him to conclude that the principles of the other religion are truer than those of his own. This, said Albo, does not mean that he is to give up his religion and adopt the other, for he must subject the other religion to the same process of investigation; he must compare the second religion with a third. If he finds the third preferable to the second, he must go on to investigate the third against a fourth, and the fourth against a fifth, and so on. The result will be, said Albo, that

> no man will be firm in his belief until he has completed his investigation of all the religions in the world and chosen one in preference to all the rest. But there is the possibility that there is a religion at the extreme end of the inhabited world which is unknown to him, and which is truer than all the rest. No man [who follows this procedure] can be saved by his belief. For he cannot have perfect faith until he has investigated all religions, and he cannot investigate all religions, as we have seen.[23]

Since in history religion has taken on an infinite variety of forms, the study of comparative religion can hardly be recommended as the method to be pursued in the search for the true religion. The result is that, regardless of our exaggerated claims, we are not *really* interested in whether or not our religion is *true* in any abstract, logical, or scientific sense. Those who claim for their religion that it is the one true religion* expect that this claim will itself be accepted as an article of faith; it is not offered as a hypothesis to be investigated by a rigorous study of comparative religion.

---

* *The Declaration on Religious Freedom* (1965) by Vatican Council II states that the Synod "believe that this one true religion subsists in the Catholic and apostolic Church. . . . Therefore, it leaves untouched the traditional Catholic doctrine on the moral duty of men and societies toward the true religion and toward the one Church of Christ." *The Documents of Vatican II*, Walter M. Abbott, gen. ed. (New York, 1966), p. 677.

To further its ecumenical purpose, and in the interest of furthering human understanding and universal respect for human dignity, Vatican Council II has, however, opened the door—several doors—for "dialogue." In "dialogues" with Christians who are the "separated brethren," spokesmen are to explain the teachings of their communions in greater depth to bring out their distinctive features. "Through such dialogue," says the *Decree on Ecumenism* (1964), "everyone gains a truer knowledge and more just appreciation of the teaching and religious life of both Communions." [24] In the *Declaration on the Relationship of the Church to Non-Christian Religions* (1965), the Vatican Council used even more positive language:

> The Catholic Church rejects nothing which is true and holy in these [non-Christian] religions. She looks with sincere respect upon those ways of conduct and of life, those rules and teachings which, though differing in many particulars from what she holds and sets forth, nevertheless often reflect a ray of that Truth which enlightens all men.[25]

Although the document goes on to add that by "the Truth" it means the truth as proclaimed by the Church, it also goes on to exhort Catholics "prudently and lovingly, through dialogue and exhortation," to "acknowledge, preserve, and promote the spiritual and moral goods" found among non-Christians.

Indeed, even the truths of atheism are not to be overlooked. In the *Pastoral Constitution on the Church in the Modern World* (1965), the Vatican Council, while "rejecting atheism, root and branch," stated that the Church

> strives to detect in the atheistic mind the hidden causes for the denial of God. Conscious of how weighty are the questions which atheism raises . . . she believes these questions ought to be examined seriously and more profoundly.[26]

Bishop James A. Pike, apparently provoked by the statement of Richard Nixon, during the 1960 presidential campaign, that anyone should be eligible for the presidency except an atheist, wrote that in his ecclesiastical life he had met many Christians who, "when it came right down to it, couldn't care less about what their faith really involved," while the atheists he had met "really cared about ultimate questions." [27] And Reinhold Niebuhr has often remarked that we owe a great deal of our social and moral progress to the work of reformers who refused to stay within the traditional religions or churches, while orthodox believers used Scripture and dogma to perpetuate slavery, economic exploitation, and other evils. We are always exposed to the temptations of self-esteem and self-righteousness, and so we do not like to acknowledge that it is sometimes the person who stands outside the church or synagogue who speaks with prophetic truth and courage. There have been secular saints as well as Christian and Jewish saints.

It is related of Rabbi Moshe Leib of Sasov that a man once said to him: "You have taught us that there is no quality and no power of man that was created to no purpose. But what purpose is served by the denial of God?" The rabbi answered as follows: "This, too, can be uplifted through deeds of charity. For if someone comes to you and asks your help, you should not turn him off with pious words, saying: 'Have faith, take your troubles to God!' You must act *as if* there were no God, as if there were only one person in all the world who could help this man—only yourself."

Locke, in *A Letter Concerning Toleration*, argued that those "who deny the being of God" ought not to be tolerated. His main reason for this judgment was that "promises, covenants, and oaths, which are the bonds of human society, can have no hold upon an atheist. The taking away of God, though but even in thought, dissolves all. . . ." [28]

Again we must appeal to common sense, to our common experience of the facts of life, which shows that Locke was wrong in thinking that promises, covenants, and oaths are the bonds of human society, and that these can have no hold on the atheist.

He was wrong on both counts. The bonds of human society are not in agreements and oaths but in the very nature of man, and in his habits of thought and feeling and conduct; and though it be a mystery, yet is it true that just as the believer may commit sins against God and nature and man, so the atheist may truly bear witness to the being of God who is the creator of nature and of man, including him who is an atheist. For we must constantly remind ourselves that though we may have beliefs founded on supernatural revelation, we may be part atheist if we do not believe that God has revealed himself also in nature, which includes the mind, heart, and body of man.

But in His natural revelation, God may be *deus absconditus*, the God Who hides Himself and yet reveals Himself in man's intelligence, in man's compassion and love, in man's justice—in his conscience. And on these qualities believers in God, fortunately for the world, hold no monopoly.

It should be shattering to our sense of religious complacency that when Adolf Eichmann took the witness stand at his trial in Jerusalem, he said that although he would not take an oath as a Christian, he would swear as a believer in God. On the other hand, we ought to find comfort in the fact that nonbelievers have served terms in prison for their conscientious objection to war.

According to the Talmud, God cries out: "If only they were to forsake Me but observe My teachings!"

4. Conscience in the First Amendment

1

Assuming that the courts would concede to Timothy Leary that his League of Spiritual Discovery is a religion, and is, therefore, entitled to the full protection of the Free Exercise Clause, does it follow that the courts would then need to exempt Leary and his followers from the criminal law prohibiting the use of marihuana and other psychedelic drugs? As we have noted, the United States Court of Appeals, in September 1967, unanimously affirmed the conviction of Leary for violation of the federal criminal statutes relating to marihuana.[1] Although the case was tried before Leary announced the formation of his new sect, at the trial he established the fact that he was, at the time charged in the indictment, a member of the Brahma-krishna sect of Hinduism, in the rituals of which marihuana plays a very important part. Since in his defense Leary relied heavily on the decision of the California Supreme Court reversing the convictions of members of the Native American Church for using peyote contrary to the state statute proscribing use of this drug, we must first examine more closely the California case.[2]

The California Supreme Court found that peyote is not technically a narcotic but is a hallucinogen, that is, a substance which produces hallucinations. Even so, the court held that the Legislature could properly prohibit its use. Had the defendants been unable to rest their defense on the Free Exercise Clause, the judgments of conviction would have been affirmed.

The court recognized the difference between *beliefs* and *acts* in cases involving religious freedom. The state may abridge practices that purport to be religious—the court cited *Reynolds v. United States*,[3] which upheld a ban on polygamy even when it is practiced as a religious duty. But, said the California court, the state may do this only when it has been demonstrated that a *compelling* state interest outweighs the defendant's interest in religious freedom. For this proposition the court rested heavily on *Sherbert v. Verner*,[4] decided by the United States Supreme Court in 1963. In this case, an employer discharged an employee because she refused to work on Saturdays. She refused because she was a Seventh-Day Adventist, a denomination that has some 400,000 members and more than 3000 churches in the United States. Since she was unable to obtain employment that did not include work on Saturdays, she applied for unemployment compensation benefits. The officials rejected her claim on the ground that she had failed to qualify under the law, which required her to accept available suitable work. They held that her religious scruples did not exempt her from this requirement of the law.

The United States Supreme Court reversed the decision of the state authorities, and held: (1) The denial of compensation benefits to a Seventh-Day Adventist will clearly have the effect of impeding the observance of this religion; the pressure upon a member to forgo observance of his or her Sabbath is unmistakable. The ruling of the state, said Justice Brennan for the Court,

> forces her to choose between following the precepts of her religion and forfeiting benefits, on the one hand, and abandoning one of the precepts of her religion in order to accept work, on

the other hand. Governmental imposition of such a choice puts the same kind of burden upon the free exercise of religion as would a fine against appellant for her Saturday worship.

The Court was thus satisfied that the denial of compensation benefits clearly constituted a burden upon the free exercise of appellant's religion. (2) But this could not be the end of the inquiry; for clearly a ban on polygamy was a burden upon the free exercise of the Mormon religion, and yet the ban was upheld. Justice Brennan therefore proceeded to consider whether some *compelling* state interest justified the substantial infringement of the First Amendment right. "It is basic," said Justice Brennan, "that no showing merely of a rational relationship to some colorable state interest would suffice; in this highly sensitive constitutional area, 'only the gravest abuses, endangering paramount interests, give occasion for permissible limitation.' " The Court found in this case no proof of such abuse or danger to warrant "a substantial infringement of religious liberties."

Now, the California Supreme Court applied the same analytical method in the peyote case: (1) Does the statute impose a burden upon the free exercise of the religion of the Native American Church? The court found on the record that the statutory prohibition most seriously infringed upon the defendant's religion—Peyotism. Peyote, said the court, "serves as a sacramental symbol similar to bread and wine in certain Christian churches," but it is more than a symbol; it is in itself an object of worship: "prayers are directed to it much as prayers are devoted to the Holy Ghost." Moreover, Peyotism considers the use of peyote for nonreligious purposes sacrilegious. Peyote must be treated with reverence, as an amulet, a protector. Just as a Catholic may wear a medallion, an Indian often wears around his neck a beautifully beaded pouch containing one large peyote button. From these and other facts, the court concluded that the prohibition of peyote would result in a virtual inhibition of the practice of the defendants' religion: "To forbid the use of peyote is to remove the theological heart of Peyotism." (2) But does not the state, nonetheless, have a "compelling state interest" that warrants the abridgement of the defendants' First Amendment right? The court held that the state had failed to demonstrate this interest. The evidence did not show that the use of peyote leads to narcotics addiction; or that Indians employ the drug in place of medical care; or that small children become addicted; or that teen-agers use peyote; or that its use works permanent injury. Indeed, the court was impressed with expert testimony that the moral standards of members of the Native American Church were higher than those of other Indians.

The court made an interesting distinction between the case before it and the polygamy law in *Reynolds*. While polygamy was a basic tenet of Mormonism, it was not, said the court, essential to the practice of the religion; peyote is, however, the *sine qua non* of the Native American Church. "It is," said the court, "the sole means by which defendants are able to experience their religion; without peyote defendants cannot practice their faith." Furthermore, in *Reynolds* the Supreme Court considered polygamy a serious threat to democratic institutions, a practice highly injurious to women involved in polygamous marriages. The Court in *Reynolds* classed polygamy with human sacrifices and the burning of widows at their husbands' funerals. The use of peyote, however, presents only slight danger to the state and to the enforcement of its narcotics laws.

The court's concluding observation is especially interesting as a recognition of the close connection between religious liberty and cultural pluralism:

> In a mass society, which presses at every point toward conformity, the protection of a self-expression, however unique, of the individual and the group becomes even more important. The varying currents of the subcultures that flow into the mainstream of our national life give it depth and beauty. We preserve a

greater value than an ancient tradition when we protect the rights of the Indians who honestly practiced an old religion in using peyote one night at a meeting in a desert hogan. . . .

2

Now let us return to the Leary case. The United States Court of Appeals also took as its point of departure the distinction between beliefs and acts, and the general proposition that religious belief will not excuse an unlawful practice. But from this point on the court moved on lines different from those of the court in the peyote case. The chief differences are notable:

(1) At the trial, Leary claimed to be a Hindu, also that marihuana was *the essence* of his religion. The Court of Appeals said that the use of marihuana is not a requisite of the practice of Hinduism. The evidence showed that only *some* Hindus use the drug as an aid to attaining consciousness expansion, so that they may more easily meditate or commune with their god. The Court of Appeals distinguished the California case by saying that the sacramental use of peyote was "the cornerstone of the peyote religion." The court then said in a footnote:

> The exemption accorded the use of peyote in the limited bona fide religious ceremonies of the relatively small, unknown Native American Church is clearly distinguishable from the private and personal use of marihuana by any person who claims he is using it as religious practice.

As we have noted, Leary was tried and convicted before he formed his own religious society. His League of Spiritual Discovery was modeled on the Native American Church in making the use of certain drugs *the essence* of religious belief and experience for its members.

It can be said that both the California and federal courts

were on the wrong track in pursuing their inquiries into what is and what is not *the essence* of a particular religion. To the early Mormons polygamy was a duty, the neglect of which would lead to eternal damnation. That would have made it important enough for members of the Mormon Church. But the Supreme Court made no special point of the essential nature and status of polygamy in Mormon beliefs.

The fact is that Mormonism has survived and even prospered without polygamy—in the last quarter of a century the Mormon Church has grown from 860,000 to 2,400,000 members.[5] Religions, like other social institutions, have ways of surviving what may at first seem like a deathblow. Judaism survived the destruction of the Jewish state and of the Temple, both of which had seemed to be absolutely indispensable. Observance of Saturday as the Sabbath is very important to Seventh-Day Adventists and to the two Seventh-Day Baptist sects (not to mention orthodox Judaism); but there are Adventists who are not *Seventh-Day* Adventists, and some twenty-five million Baptists who believe that Sunday, not the seventh day, is the holy Sabbath day. One man will place the emphasis on his being an Adventist or a Baptist, while another Adventist or Baptist will place the emphasis on observance of the seventh day— and no court can say that either is guilty of misplaced emphasis.

Maimonides made a list of thirteen principles that he considered fundamental to Judaism. But Hasdai Crescas found only six fundamental principles, and made up a list of eight others which he considered true beliefs but not of a fundamental nature. Albo in turn found only three basic dogmas, but then also had a list of eight beliefs which he considered to be not fundamental but derivative principles.[6] Maimonides held that the dogma of the Messiah was a fundamental principle, but Albo thought that one could conceive of the Torah of Moses without it. He noted, however, that belief in the Messiah was a special principle of the Christians, "for *their* religion cannot exist without it." [7] One could go on and on with this sort of history of the dogmas of any major religion. Today, even theologians tend to find more fruitful fields for cultivation. It is impossible to see how American courts could possibly permit themselves to investigate theological mysteries. In *The Praise of Folly* Erasmus said of theologians that they are

> protected by a wall of scholastic definitions, arguments, corollaries, implicit and explicit propositions; they have so many hideaways that they could not be caught even by the net of Vulcan; for they slip out on their distinctions. . . .[8]

Albo and Erasmus were near contemporaries. Would Erasmus have agreed with Albo that Christianity would collapse without a belief in the coming (or second coming) of the Messiah?

For a court to try to distinguish between the "essence" of a man's religion and what in his religion is outside of its "essence" is to define what another may label orthodox or heretical.

(2) The Court of Appeals refused to go into the question whether marihuana is *in fact* a harmful drug. Leary had introduced evidence at his trial that the drug is harmless; the Court of Appeals held that the evidence was not pertinent, and that the government was not required to controvert Leary's witnesses on this "controversial question." It was enough for the court that "Congress has demonstrated beyond doubt [by making traffic in marihuana a crime subject to severe penalties] that it believes marihuana is an evil in American society and a serious threat to its people."

But the court must have forgotten that our complex of statutory penalties is a hodgepodge of prejudice, ignorance, indifference, bungling, confusion, and sheer stupidity. The severity of a penalty provided by a statute may be a surer mark of the absence of reason going into the framing and adoption of the act than its presence; for often it is a clear expression of sheer vindictiveness. (Many of our courts today try to compensate for this by taking a more rational, objective view of the crime and the offender at the time of sentencing; but in the Leary case the imposition of a thirty-year prison sentence and a $30,000 fine chiefly for transportation of three ounces of marihuana—with no implication that Leary was engaged in the commercial handling of the drug for private profit—was outrageously unjust and could only be an expression of a meanly vindictive spirit.)

In any case, the Court of Appeals was simply willing to assume, without a serious investigation, that "Congress has demonstrated beyond doubt that it believes marihuana is an evil in American society and a serious threat to its people." Even if Congress in fact did believe this, such belief on the part of Congress is not conclusive on the constitutional issue—not by any means. We have on our books many laws that unmistakably express the firm conviction of Congress that the Communist Party and Communist front organizations are serious threats and menaces to the security of the United States—a matter of far greater importance than the transportation of marihuana; yet in case after case the Supreme Court went into the question whether the known facts concerning these organizations would be sufficient to uphold the statutory structure built on them by Congress in its attempts to expose, restrict, or punish Communist Party officials or members.[9]

In the opinion of the Court of Appeals, the only words that attempt to rationalize its position on this point are these:

It would be difficult to imagine the harm which would result if the criminal statutes against marihuana were nullified as to those who claim the right to possess and traffic in this drug for religious purposes. For all practical purposes the anti-marihuana laws would be meaningless, and enforcement impossible. The danger is too great, especially to the youth of the nation, at a time when psychedelic experience, "turn on," is the "in" thing to so many, for this court to yield to the argument that the use of marihuana for *so-called* religious purposes should be permitted under the Free Exercise Clause. We will not, therefore, subscribe to the *dangerous* *doctrine* that the free exercise of religion accords an unlimited freedom to violate the laws of the land relative to marihuana. [Italics supplied.]

First of all, the court had no business belittling Leary's religious claims by referring to his "so-called religious purposes." Even in the polygamy cases the Supreme Court treated the religious claims of the Mormons—and this was a hundred years ago, long before Mormonism became respectable and an accepted part of the American scene—with more deference.

But what is much more consequential is that this whole argument of the court rests on the proposition that marihuana is *in fact* a dangerous drug, that it is *in fact* "an evil in American society and a serious threat to its people." This proposition the court did not, and would not, examine; it merely assumed it as an indubitable truth—as if it were a dogma of the court's own religion! Yet it is at the very heart of the controversy.

The essential steps for the court to have taken were two: (1) Was there *in fact* a compelling social interest that warranted Congress in prohibiting traffic in marihuana? What is the *evidence* that marihuana is *in fact* an evil and a threat, such as would warrant congressional action through the criminal-law process? To let Congress act as the *sole judge* of this issue would mean the end of judicial review of legislation that might be constitutionally questionable. Our courts have given no indication of any move toward this end. Although the Supreme Court acts more reluctantly today than it did before 1937 in judicial review of federal legislation, the record since then hardly shows that the Court has surrendered this power.[10] (2) If it were established to the satisfaction of the court that Congress had been warranted in finding a compelling social interest in prohibiting traffic in marihuana, the court would then need to go into the question of whether the refusal to exempt Leary on religious grounds would be constitutionally warranted. In the case of the Seventh-Day Adventist, the Court said that in the "highly sensitive constitutional area" of religious liberty, "only the gravest abuses, endangering paramount interests, give occasion for permissible limitation." In that case, the state argued that the exemption of Seventh-Day observers from the requirement to work on Saturdays would create administrative difficulties and would create the possibility of filing fraudulent claims by unscrupulous claimants of unemployment compensation, "feigning religious objections to Saturday work." But the Supreme Court found that the record did not sustain these arguments. There was, said the Court,

> no proof whatever to warrant such fears of malingering or deceit.
> . . . Even if consideration of such evidence is not foreclosed by the prohibition against judicial inquiry into the truth or falsity of religious beliefs, United States v. Ballard—question as to which we intimate no view since it is not before us—it is highly doubtful whether such evidence would be sufficient to warrant a substantial infringement of religious liberties. For even if the possibility of spurious claims did threaten to dilute the fund and disrupt the scheduling of work, it would plainly be incumbent upon the [state] to demonstrate that no alternative forms of regulation would combat such abuses without infringing First Amendment rights.[11]

In the Leary case the court simply and cavalierly brushed aside these highly significant questions.

The court's action does not, however, put to sleep the highly controversial question as to the propriety of the prohibition of marihuana. It is hard to believe that the Court of Appeals did not know of the growing body of respectable professional opinion which holds that there is no justification for putting this drug in the class with such hard-core habit-forming drugs as heroin, morphine, and opium. There are those who would legalize the sale and use of marihuana as that of alcoholic beverages has been, that is, subject its sale to some legal regulation; others would remove all restrictions. Critics of the present criminal law argue that, in any case, alcoholic beverages and cigarette smoking are much more habit-forming and are greater menaces to welfare, health, and even life, and that aspirin, which can readily be purchased even in grocery shops, kills more people each year than any other available drug. The controversy also brings up a point considered in John Stuart Mill's essay *On Liberty*, in which the position is forcefully maintained that self-regarding conduct—including gambling, drunkenness, and idleness—is beyond the legitimate sphere of governmental action; that for the violation of a duty to one's self a person should not be accountable to the state.[12] This is an argument that today would be embraced within the concept of "privacy." * Whatever the merits of the debate over the effects of marihuana or of Mill's position as it may involve the right to use this drug, a court cannot excuse itself from entering these debates once the defendant, as did Timothy Leary, raises the defense of the Free Exercise Clause and introduces or offers to introduce evidence on the effects of the drug.**

3

We have called attention to another distinction found by the court in the Leary case to mark it off from the peyote case in California; namely, that the latter involved the use of peyote in the religious ceremonies of an identifiable, though "relatively small and unknown" church, while the Leary use involved "the

* The Wolfenden Report, *Report of the Committee on Homosexual Offences and Prostitution* (London 1957), and other recent proposals with respect to sexual acts seem to reflect Mill's approach and probably also his influence.
** On June 10, 1968, the Supreme Court granted the petition for writ of certiorari, limited, however, to the question whether the registration and tax provisions of the narcotics law as applied to Leary violated his privilege against self-incrimination, and whether he was denied due process by the provision in the law that an inference may be drawn respecting the illegal origin and nature of marihuana solely from possession thereof. *Leary v. United States*, 88 S. Ct. 2058. On May 19, 1969, the conviction was reversed on both grounds.

private and personal use of marihuana by [a] person who claims he is using it as a religious practice."

This distinction seems to be constitutionally unwarranted. On the facts, Leary produced evidence that he was a member of the Brahmakrishna sect of Hinduism, in which marihuana plays a very important part, and this evidence was not controverted by the prosecution's witnesses. But beyond this, whatever the situation may have been centuries ago, how can the Free Exercise Clause be limited to benefit only *institutionalized* religions?

For one thing, many of the religions we know today had their origin in a "private and personal" religious experience. Mohammed did not take over an on-going, established religion; the history of Islam records the names of his first three converts. John Wesley is given credit as the founder of Methodism. Mrs. Mary Baker Eddy was the founder of the Christian Science church. Menno Simons organized a division of Anabaptists that in due course became the sect known as the Mennonites. Jacob Ammon broke away from the Mennonites and founded the sect known as the Amish. Before there is a history of a church, there is the biography of a man. "I do not," wrote Thomas Paine in *The Age of Reason,*

> believe in the creed professed by the Jewish church, by the Roman church, by the Greek church, by the Turkish church, by the Protestant church, nor by any church that I know of. My own mind is my own church.

The founder of almost every religion, no matter how solid and massive and respectable it may be today, could have made such a claim at one time. I think it was Bronson Alcott who said that he belonged to the Church of One Member. This could have been said at one time by George Fox, before he found followers who later became the Society of Friends. In one form or another it is today being said by countless persons throughout the United States and Europe. They seem to agree with Emerson that

In the Bible you are not directed to be a Unitarian, or a Calvinist or an Episcopalian. Now if a man is wise, he will not only not profess himself to be a Unitarian, but he will say to himself, I am not a member of that or of any [religious] party [sect]. . . . Socrates, Aristotle, Calvin, Luther . . . what are these but names of parties? Which is to say, as fast as we use our own eyes, we quit these parties or Unthinking Corporations, and join ourselves to God in an unpartaken relation.

In fact, Emerson—and he is representative of many others—thought that religion and sectarianism were contradictories. For religion, he held, is "the relation of the soul to God, and therefore the progress of Sectarianism marks the decline of religion." [13] In his essay "The Over-Soul," which has been read by and has influenced countless Americans since its publication in 1841, Emerson wrote:

The soul makes no appeal from itself. Our religion vulgarly stands on numbers of believers. Whenever the appeal is made—no matter how indirectly—to numbers, proclamation is then and there made, that religion is not. He that finds God a sweet, enveloping thought to him, never counts his company. . . . It makes no difference whether the appeal is to numbers or to one. . . . Great is the soul, and plain. It is no flatterer, it is no follower; it never appeals from itself.

Must religion—as the term is used in the First Amendment—be organized into a sect and a church before it will be protected by the Free Exercise Clause? Emerson would have rejected the suggestion. His friend Thoreau asked, "What is religion?" and himself answered: "That which is never spoken." In this he shared company with George Fox, whose mystical experience in 1646 taught him that Christianity is not an outward profession but an inner light by which God directly illumines the soul. What Thoreau objected to in the religion he saw about him was precisely that it was public. His own religion, he said, had to be "as unpublic and incommunicable" as his spirit of poetry, and to be approached "with as much love and tenderness." [14] Quakers do not have churches but meeting houses, and the Old Order Amish do not use churches but worship in homes.

Thomas Jefferson, whose spirit speaks through the Religion Clauses of the First Amendment, would have been at home with Alcott, Emerson, and Thoreau; for Jefferson insisted that his religious belief was a very personal, strictly private matter. His rule was, he wrote to John Adams, to "say nothing of my religion. It is known to my God and myself alone." Indeed, with respect to sects and churches, Jefferson took a strongly negative position. If, he wrote in another letter to Adams,

> by religion, we are to understand *Sectarian dogmas*, in which no two of them agree, then your exclamation on that hypothesis is just, "that this would be the best of all possible worlds, if there were no religion in it." [15]

Thus, what the Court of Appeals in the Leary case rejected as merely private and personal, others might select and honor as the innermost heart of that which the Free Exercise Clause projects. It matters not constitutionally whether a church has a million members or is a Church of One Member; whether it has thirteen fundamental principles, or six, or one; whether its members hold a service or a meeting; whether they come together in a church or synagogue or in a home; whether they listen to hymns and prayers or simply sit and meditate and listen to the inner voice and see only the inner light. As to this church or that, as to this religion or that, the Constitution, in the spirit of the Voice addressed to the disputing rabbis of the Talmud, says: "The words of both are the words of the Living God. . . ."

4

This brings us to that which is, for modern man, the source and depository, the energy and agency of religion—the personal, individual conscience. When we speak of freedom of religion, we tend to think of freedom of churches, freedom of organized, institutionalized religions. This is, of course, an important aspect of the meaning of the Religion Clauses in the First Amendment, and the long sweep of history up to a few centuries ago justifies this concentration on the *public* aspect of religion; for religions, and even the gods, were conceived of as attached to particular peoples, nations, tribes, and lands.

While these links remain, the *private aspects*—religion as the voice of the *individual conscience*—have assumed at least equal importance. The idea of the *privacy* of the religious conscience is not, of course, altogether new. Socrates spoke of it in his address to the Athenian jury that tried and convicted him, and to his friends who called on him in prison. The great Stoic philosophers, especially Epictetus and Marcus Aurelius, who sharply marked off the realm of the private from the realm of the public, knew and greatly valued its existence. It was, however, in the late seventeenth century and more widely in the eighteenth century that philosophy and religious thought seemed to have discovered the *locus* of religion and religious feeling in the sphere of the private, in "the still small voice" that speaks to the soul. Philosophers such as Shaftesbury, Francis Hutcheson, and Richard Price tended to build moral theories on conscience as a mental or volitional faculty; but these theories are not our present concern. What is our concern is that by the beginning of the nineteenth century it was perfectly natural for Thomas Jefferson to write:

> We are bound, you, I, and every one, to make common cause . . . to maintain the common right of freedom of conscience.[16]

For freedom of religion to Jefferson had come to mean freedom of the mind; insofar as it concerned *public law*, religion was to be regarded—and guarded—as a wholly *private matter*, a matter of private conscience.[17]

Now, with this background in mind, let us examine one more recent decision of the United States Supreme Court, the extremely instructive case of *United States v. Seeger*, decided in 1965.[18] The case involved a provision of the Universal Military Training and Service Act of 1948,[19] which, as a prerequisite of exempting a conscientious objector from military service, requires him to show that "by reason of religious training and belief," he is "conscientiously opposed to participation in war in any form," and defines "religious training and belief" in the following terms:

> Religious training and belief in this connection means an individual's belief in a relation to a Supreme Being involving duties superior to those arising from any human relation, but does not include essentially political, sociological, or philosophical views or a merely personal moral code.

We should note in passing that this definition of "religious training and belief" is taken mainly from Chief Justice Hughes's dissenting opinion in *United States v. Macintosh*,[20] which we discussed earlier. But the Congress made one significant change from the words of Chief Justice Hughes: it substituted "Supreme Being" for "God." Ironically, the term chosen by Congress, as we saw earlier, was that used by Robespierre and by Auguste Comte!

The Seeger case involved three men who had been denied status as conscientious objectors:

Daniel A. Seeger claimed that he was conscientiously opposed to participation in war in any form by reason of his "religious belief" but said that he preferred to leave open the question of his belief in a Supreme Being. While admitting to skepticism or disbelief in the existence of God, he avowed a "belief in and devotion to goodness and virtue for their own sakes, and a religious faith in a purely ethical creed." He cited Plato, Aristotle, and Spinoza for support of his ethical belief in intellectual and moral integrity "without belief in God, except in the remotest sense."

The second man, Arno S. Jakobson, explained that his religious and social thinking had developed after meditation and thought. He reached the conclusion, he said, that man was partly spiritual and was, therefore, "partly akin to the Supreme Reality." He defined religion as the "sum and essence of one's basic attitudes to the fundamental problems of human existence"; and he said that he believed in "Godness," which was "the Ultimate Cause for the fact of the Being of the Universe." He said that one could be related to "Godness" vertically or horizontally, that is, through mankind and the world, and that he accepted the latter.

The third man, Forest B. Peter, said that he belonged to no sect or organization; that he approved of John Haynes Holmes's definition of religion as "the consciousness of some power manifest in nature which helps man in the ordering of his life in harmony with its demands . . . [it] is the supreme expression of human nature; it is man thinking his highest, feeling his deepest, and living his best." He traced the source of his conviction to reading and meditation "in our democratic American culture, with its values derived from the western religious and philosophical tradition." As to his belief in a Supreme Being, Peter said that he supposed "you could call that a belief in the Supreme Being or God. These just do not happen to be the words I use."

In his opinion for the Court, which decided unanimously in favor of the three conscientious objectors, Justice Clark recalled that the dissenting opinion of Chief Justice Hughes in *Macintosh* had given the rationale for recognition of conscientious objection to war in his statement that "in the forum of conscience, duty to a moral power higher than the State has always been maintained"; and that Chief Justice Stone had written the following:

Both morals and sound policy require that the state should not violate the conscience of the individual. All our history gives confirmation to the view that liberty of conscience has a moral and social value which makes it worthy of preservation at the hands of the state. So deep in its significance and vital, indeed, is it to the integrity of man's moral and spiritual nature that nothing short of the self-preservation of the state should warrant its violation; and it may well be questioned whether the state which preserves its life by a settled policy of violation of the conscience of the individual will not in fact ultimately lose it by the process.[21]

The Court noted that the Draft Act of 1917 afforded exemptions to conscientious objectors who were affiliated with a well-recognized religious sect whose creed forbade its members to participate in war in any form. The conscription act of 1940 broadened the exemption by moving away from membership in a pacifist sect to "religious training and belief." Between the two world wars Congress had come to recognize that a person may be religious without belonging to an organized church, just as minority members of a nonpacifist faith might, "through religious reading," reach a pacifist position. (Seeger had been brought up in a devout Roman Catholic home, but derived his pacifism from a study of Quaker beliefs.) "Indeed," Justice Clark noted,

the consensus of the witnesses appearing before the congressional committees was that individual belief—rather than membership in a church or sect—determined the duties that God imposed upon a person in his everyday conduct; and that "there is a higher loyalty than loyalty to this country, loyalty to God."

The phrase "religious training and belief," then, can mean the faith of a pacifist who belongs to a nonpacifist church, one who, in fact, chooses to act in opposition to the position on war taken by his own church. The phrase means also the faith of a pacifist who belongs to the Church of One Member.

Congress, however, excluded two classes of persons: (1)

those who oppose war on the basis of "essentially political, sociological, or philosophical views," and (2) pacifists whose position is founded on "a merely personal moral code." On the first point, Justice Clark stated that considerations as to war that are essentially political, sociological, or philosophical "have historically been reserved for the Government." With respect to such judgments, the conviction of the individual cannot override that of the state. What the Court meant, it seems, is that when one makes a political, sociological, or philosophical—or economic—judgment on war, disassociating that judgment from religious belief, or at the same time disavowing religious belief, then he cannot claim exemption on the statutory ground of religious training and belief.

Now, while one can recognize the possibility of subtle psychological and emotional difficulties in this differentiation between religious belief and political, sociological, or philosophical judgment, the Court here is on firm constitutional ground, for the First Amendment gives a special place to religious belief but not to political or other kinds of judgment.

The Court was not deciding the case on the basis of the First Amendment but on a construction of the language of the Universal Military Training and Service Act. By finding for the three conscientious objectors, the Court was able to by-pass the constitutional issue; but surely, always in the background, the Free Exercise Clause threw its shadow over the case, and Justice Douglas, in his separate opinion, was right in pointing out that a decision other than that reached by the Court would have violated the Free Exercise Clause.

In the case before the Court, Justice Clark was able to point out that all three men claimed that their pacifism was based on "religious training and belief." No one among them claimed to be an atheist. Nor, said the Court, do the men avow monotheism or any other seemingly orthodox faith. Well, but what did Congress mean by the term "Supreme Being"? In trying to answer this question, the Court found itself facing some of the most explosive questions ever presented to a court. Still, the question put in the form of statutory construction rather than constitutional interpretation made the Court's task a bit easier —though again one must remember that the constitutional issue could not altogether be absent from the minds of the Justices.

Before exploring the statutory meaning of "Supreme Being," one should ask how those who claim conscientious objection to war on the basis of a "merely personal moral code" were excluded. The Court simply noted that each claimant in the case based his pacifism on a religious belief. Since religious belief, as we have seen, need not be that of an organized church or sect, it may be, of course, purely personal, that of the Church of One Member. The only requirement imposed by Congress is that the belief—though personal and not necessarily organizational—be related to a Supreme Being, and thus be *religious*. If it is that, it meets the statutory test and is not, then, a belief based on a "merely personal *moral* code." Although Congress did not recognize a "merely personal moral code," it did recognize a merely personal religious code—provided only that the code or belief was related to a Supreme Being.*

5

What, then, did Congress mean by a Supreme Being? Justice Clark first pointed out how pluralistic in its religious beliefs American society has become. Considering only the historical pacifist churches, the Court noted that there were four denominations using the name Friends, four denominations of those commonly called Brethren, and seventeen denominations grouped as Mennonite bodies. Congress, recognizing the magnitude of the problem and wishing to avoid picking and choos-

* See page ix.

ing among religious beliefs, purposely substituted "Supreme Being" for "God" in taking over Chief Justice Hughes's definition of religion. By failing to define "Supreme Being," Congress must have been mindful of Hughes's admonition:

> Putting aside dogmas with their particular conceptions of deity, freedom of conscience itself implies respect for an innate conviction of paramount duty. The battle for religious liberty has been fought and won with respect to religious beliefs and practices, which are not in conflict with good order, upon the very ground of the supremacy of conscience within its proper field.

All that is required, said the Court, is "a conviction based upon religious training and belief." What comes within the meaning of this phrase? "Within that phrase," said the Court, could come

> all sincere religious beliefs which are based upon a power or being, or upon a faith, to which all else is subordinate or upon which all else is ultimately dependent. The test might be stated in these words: A sincere and meaningful belief which occupies in the life of its possessor a place parallel to that filled by the God of those admittedly qualifying for the exemption comes within the statutory definition. This construction avoids imputing to Congress an intent to classify different religious beliefs, exempting some and excluding others, and is in accord with the well-established congressional policy of equal treatment for those whose opposition to service is grounded in their religious tenets.

There was no evidence, said Justice Clark, that Congress intended to restrict the concept of religious belief, to make it available only to those believing in a traditional God.

Moreover, said the Court, its construction of the statutory language embraces "the ever-broadening understanding of the modern religious community." Here the Court referred to and quoted from the writings of contemporary theologians.[22] Paul Tillich, the Court pointed out, identified God, not as a projection "out there" or beyond the skies, but as the ground of our very being. The Court quoted from Tillich's *Systematic Theology:*

> I have written of the God above the God of theism. . . . In such a state [of self-affirmation] the God of both religious and theological language disappears. But something remains, namely, the seriousness of that doubt in which meaning within meaninglessness is affirmed. The source of this affirmation of meaning within meaninglessness, of certitude within doubt, is not the God of traditional theism but the "God above God," the power of being, which works through those who have no name for it, not even the name of God.

The Court also quoted from *Honest to God* by John A. T. Robinson, Bishop of Woolwich, as follows:

> The Bible speaks of a God "up there." No doubt its picture of a three decker universe, of "the heaven above, the earth beneath and the waters under the earth," was once taken quite literally. . . . [Later] in place of a God who is literally or physically "up there" we have accepted, as part of our mental furniture, a God who is spiritually or metaphysically "out there." But now it seems there is no room for him, not merely in the inn, but in the entire universe: for there are no vacant places left. In reality, of course, our new view of the universe has made not the slightest difference. . . .
>
> But the idea of a God spiritually or metaphysically "out there" dies very much harder. Indeed most people would be seriously disturbed by the thought that it should need to die at all. For it *is* their God and they have nothing to put in its place. . . . Everyone of us lives with some mental picture of a God "out there," a God who exists above and beyond the world he made, a God "to" whom we pray and to whom we "go" when we die. But the signs are that we are reaching the point at which the whole conception of God "out there," which has served us so well since the collapse of the three decker universe is becoming more a hindrance than a help.

Significantly, the Court quoted the following passage from *Ethics As a Religion* (1951) by David Saville Muzzey, a leader in the Ethical Culture Movement:

Instead of positing a personal God, whose existence man can neither prove nor disprove, the ethical concept is founded on human experience. It is anthropocentric, not theocentric. Religion, for all the various definitions that have been given of it, must surely mean the devotion of man to the highest ideal that he can conceive. And that ideal is a community of spirits in which the latent moral potentialities of men shall have been elicited by their reciprocal endeavors to cultivate the best in their fellow men. What ultimate reality is we do not know; but we have the faith that expresses itself in the human world as the power which inspires in man moral purposes. . . .

Thus the "God" that we love is not the figure on the great white throne, but the perfect pattern, envisioned by faith, of humanity as it should be, purged of the evil elements which retard its progress toward "the knowledge, love and practice of the right."

Certainly these words are not in essence different from those used by Chaumette or Comte when they wrote about the Religion of Humanity. To them, and to Muzzey, it made no difference whether their beliefs were described as constituting a religious belief or a moral code. At some point, as in the influential thought of Matthew Arnold, morality became religion or religion became morality.

But this can be said also of some well-established religions. When the prophet Micah said,

What doth the Lord require of thee, but to do justly, and to love mercy, and to walk humbly with thy God? (Mic. 6–8)

or when Isaiah said,

Is it such a fast that I have chosen? a day for a man to afflict his soul? . . . Is not this the fast that I have chosen? to loose the bands of wickedness, to undo the heavy burdens, and to let the oppressed go free, and that ye break every yoke? (Isa. 58:5–6)

were they able to say where religion ended and morality began? Indeed, there is no word for religion in biblical Hebrew. There is *kodesh*, meaning sacred or holy, but the term is also used in connection with profane and even obscene actions and persons. Nor is there a word for religion in classical Greek or Latin, but only such ambiguous terms as *hiera* and *sacra*.

The Court in *Seeger* was able to avoid tangling with such questions because each of the three conscientious objectors said that his position was based on religious belief. They used the statutory formula. Perhaps they meant what they said. But one may wonder whether the statute did not in fact suggest to them the talismanic words they were required to use if they were to qualify as conscientious objectors. Consciously or unconsciously, they may have regarded the words of the statute as a form of magical mumbo jumbo. Although the words used by each of the men differ from those used by the others, the statutory test, said the Court, "is simple of application. It is essentially," the opinion went on to say, "an objective one, namely,

does the claimed belief occupy the same place in the life of the objector as an orthodox belief in God holds in the life of one clearly qualified for exemption?

The Court, in effect, was saying that if a man speaks and conducts himself *as if* he had conscientious objection to war in any form based on religious belief, then he comes within the statutory classification. This is obviously a practical, pragmatic approach to an otherwise hopelessly complex and perhaps insoluble problem. Maybe this is as much as we have a right to ask. The Court, summarizing Seeger's position, said: "We think it clear that the beliefs which prompted his objection occupy the same place in his life as the belief in a traditional deity holds in the lives of his friends, the Quakers"; and then the Court added that it was reminded once more of Paul Tillich's thoughts, as expressed in *The Shaking of the Foundations:*

And if that word [God] has not much meaning for you, translate it, and speak of your life, of the source of your being, of your ultimate concern, *of what you take seriously without any reservation.* Perhaps, in order to do so, you must forget every-thing traditional that you have learned about God. [Emphasis supplied.]

This means that the law will recognize as a religious belief a man's faith even though it involves his forgetting everything traditional that he had ever learned about God. This in turn means that the term "religion," as it is used in the First Amend-ment, is one that cannot be defined; it remains ever open-ended to receive another, and still another, and ever still another new faith, new denomination, new church, new Church of One Member.

Concurring, Justice Douglas drew this constitutional con-clusion and stated it formally:

If I read the statute differently from the Court, I would have difficulties. For then those who embraced one religious faith rather than another would be subject to penalties; and that kind of discrimination, as we held in *Sherbert* v. *Verner*, would violate the Free Exercise Clause of the First Amendment. It would also result in a denial of equal protection by preferring some religions over others—an invidious discrimination that would run afoul of the Due Process Clause of the Fifth Amend-ment.

It is paradoxical, however, that the Free Exercise Clause, which was intended to give maximum liberty to religion, should become in a way a snare for the conscience. In granting exemp-tion to conscientious objectors whose pacifism is founded on their religious beliefs, Congress was obviously attempting to meet the words of the First Amendment. (This does not mean that the Free Exercise Clause *compels* Congress to exempt conscientious objectors. The Supreme Court has never said this.[23]) The exclusion of a personal moral code and of philo-sophical, political, and sociological grounds for conscientious objection underscores the intent of Congress to limit exemption to those with religious beliefs. The effect of the statutory provision is to influence conscientious objectors consciously or unconsciously to dress up their convictions in the language of the act, to use formulas that will minimize their troubles.

At the very end of the Court's opinion appears this brief paragraph:

> It will be remembered that Peter acknowledged "some power manifest in nature . . . the supreme expression" that helps man in ordering his life. As to whether he would call that belief in a Supreme Being, he replied, "You could call that a belief in the Supreme Being or God. Those just do not happen to be words I use." We think that under the test we establish here the Board would grant the exemption to Peter.

It seems that both Peter and the Court were straining at a gnat and swallowing a camel.* Men and courts sometimes need to do this, for the law has its forms and formalities and yet does not wish to sacrifice substantive justice to them. But this process is distasteful, and even reprehensible, where what is involved is a matter of conscience. Once more words of Thomas Jefferson come to mind:

> Compulsion in religion is distinguished peculiarly from compulsion in every other thing. I may grow rich by an art I am compelled to follow, I may recover health by medicines I am compelled to take against my own judgment, but I cannot be saved by a *worship* I disbelieve.[24]

6

If Jefferson and Madison had had foreknowledge of events in our country, they might have framed the Religion Clauses a little differently:

* See page x.

Congress shall make no law respecting an establishment of religion, or prohibiting the free exercise thereof [or of conscience].

This enlargement would have saved us much trouble. We would
not have needed to worry over whether Ethical Culture or
humanism is a religion, or whether the pacifism of a Seeger or a
Peter is based on religious belief. For at the heart of the beliefs
of such men and movements is conscience; and persons who
avow religious beliefs—fortunately for mankind—do not hold a
monopoly on conscience. If there is one thing that a Jehovah's
Witness, a vegetarian,[25] and a Quaker may have in common
when they register as conscientious objectors to war, it is that
each man's conscience compels him to say to the authorities, in
the words of Luther: *Hier stehe ich! Ich kann nicht anders*
"Here I stand. I cannot do otherwise."

Although Congress and the courts have thus far failed to give
constitutional or statutory dignity to conscience where its claims
are projected clear of the religious formula, other agencies in
our day have selected conscience for the highest position in any
order of values. Indeed, we may say that at no time in history
has conscience received as much recognition as it has since the
Second World War. To note only three of the most significant
events or actions on this point:

First, the Nuremberg trials of Nazi war leaders in 1945–1946
established the principle in international law that the defense
of having acted pursuant to orders of the government or a superior officer does not absolve a defendant from responsibility.
This principle was confirmed by the trials of the Japanese war
leaders in 1946–1947, and by several thousand other trials in
various national courts. The principle is now well-established in
the law and is included in the instructions on warfare issued
for their military forces by the United States and Great Britain,
and is included also in the Draft Code of Offences Against the
Peace and Security of Mankind, prepared by the International
Law Commission and submitted to the United Nations General
Assembly.

The essence of the Nuremberg principle is that every soldier, every officer, every man—Christian, Jew, Hindu, Moslem, pagan, atheist—must conduct himself on the belief that he has moral duties "superior to those arising from any human relation." The Nuremberg tribunal was not interested in the "religion" of any Nazi defendant, nor did it care whether he believed in God or in a Supreme Being. It was enough that the defendants were men.

The Constitution of the U.S.S.R. gives special recognition to antireligious propaganda. Russian society today may be predominantly atheistic. If a Russian atheist were charged with crimes against humanity under the Nuremberg precedents— for inhumane acts against a civilian population, or for persecutions on political, religious, or racial grounds in connection with a war crime—would an international court accept his defense that, as he was an atheist, as he had no belief in any Supreme Being except the Soviet state, he recognized no "duties superior to those arising from any human relation," and was, therefore, bound to carry out orders from his superior officers? This is unthinkable. It would mean making atheism a sanctuary for men who would commit the most shocking atrocities. The court would be bound to reject the defense and say to the defendant: "In this court we are not interested in your religious or antireligious professions. You are a man. Your conscience should have told you that you were bound to disobey orders to commit crimes against humanity."

The second relevant development is the adoption, in 1948, of the Universal Declaration of Human Rights, by the General Assembly of the United Nations. Article 1 provides that

> All human beings are born free and equal in dignity and rights. *They are endowed with reason and conscience* and should act towards one another in a spirit of brotherhood. [Italics supplied.]

Article 18 provides that "Everyone has the right to freedom of thought, conscience and religion." This article does not duplicate Article 1, for it becomes clear from the rest of Article 18 that it pertains largely to religion. The remainder reads as follows:

> this right includes freedom to change his religion or belief, and freedom, either alone or in community with others and in public or private, to manifest his religion or belief in teaching, practice, worship and observance.

Thus, the Declaration gives separate recognition of conscience apart from its relation to religion.

The third development is the recognition of conscience by Vatican Council II.

In the *Pastoral Constitution on the Church in the World* (1965), the keynote is human dignity, which every man has in consequence of his creation "in the image of God." At the core of man made in the image of God is conscience. In the depths of his conscience man hears the voice of God, obedience to which is "the very dignity of man." It is, then, by virtue of his conscience that man is in the image of God. According to the way he obeys his conscience, he will be judged.

This is not to say that conscience never errs. But conscience, even when it is in error, does not lose its dignity.[26]

There is a universal natural law, says the *Pastoral Constitution*, whose force binds permanently; and man's conscience gives "ever more emphatic voice" to the principles of the natural law. Therefore,

> actions which deliberately conflict with these same principles, as well as orders commanding such actions, are criminal. Blind obedience cannot excuse those who yield to them. Among such must first be counted those actions designed for the methodical extermination of an entire people, nation, or ethnic minority. These actions must be vehemently condemned as horrendous crimes. The courage of those who openly and fearlessly resist men who issue such commands merits supreme commendation.[27]

The *Pastoral Constitution* also states that the law should make "humane provisions for the case of those who for reasons of

conscience refuse to bear arms," provided they accept some alternative form of service to the community.[28]

Although the document purports to state "teaching already
accepted in the Church," it is nonetheless true that the emphasis
on conscience is a recovery of a teaching that had for centuries
been ignored or even spurned. The teaching of Saint Thomas
Aquinas was that conscience binds absolutely. To act against
one's conscience is to sin. Acting against conscience is always
evil. For conscience—rightly or wrongly—declares that a certain
action is commanded by God. If a man decides to disobey it,
he sins; for he determines at that point to disobey God—or what
he believes is the will of God. Of course conscience may be in
error, and a man is commanded to examine his conscience and
what it commands with great care; but unless the judgment of
conscience is reversed, it is binding. If in fact his conscience was
in error, he will be punished for his act, but not for obeying
his conscience. If his conscience was in error but he chose to
disobey his conscience while believing its command to be God's,
then he will be punished—not, of course, for failing to do the
wrong commanded by conscience, but for acting in a way that
he believed to be disobedient to the will of God.[29]

It is the force of this Thomistic belief and logic that one now
finds renewed by the *Pastoral Constitution*, with the link it
finds between human dignity and conscience. Because the post-
Reformation era made "private judgment" so important for
Protestant development, the Roman Catholic Church generally
avoided recognition of the Thomistic teaching on conscience.
But now conscience has been given a position of highest honor
and importance: "To obey it is the very dignity of man; according to it he will be judged." [30]

Since every man, believer or nonbeliever, is made in the
image of God, every man has human dignity, and a conscience
that purports to him, rightly or wrongly, to be the voice of God.
This at least is how the believer reads the facts. Everyone, there-

fore, believer or nonbeliever, has a conscience that has the power to impose on him duties "superior to those arising from any human relation." He owes supreme allegiance to the commands of his conscience. It is not, therefore, a question of "religion" or "religious belief" or belief in any relation to a Supreme Being or God. It is entirely a matter of human dignity and conscience. A believer, then, must affirm of his nonbelieving neighbor that he, too, is made in the image of God, and that he, too, has a conscience, which has its rights and its duties.

A century ago, Cardinal Newman put the argument for the priority of conscience forcefully in answer to Gladstone's charge that Roman Catholics could not, owing to the definition of papal infallibility, be loyal citizens. When God became Creator, Newman wrote,

> He implanted this [ethical] Law, which is Himself, in the intelligence of all His rational creatures. The Divine Law, then, is the rule of ethical truth, the standard of right and wrong, a sovereign, irreversible, absolute authority . . . is called "conscience"; and, though it may suffer refraction in passing into the intellectual medium of each, it is not thereby so affected as to lose its character of being the Divine Law, but still has, as such, the prerogative of commanding obedience. "The Divine Law," Says Cardinal Gousset, "is the supreme rule of actions; our thoughts, desires, words, acts, all that man is, is subject to the domain of the law of God; and this law is the rule of conduct by means of our conscience. Hence it is never lawful to go against our conscience. . . ." I will drink to the Pope, if you please, still, to conscience first, and to the Pope afterwards.[31]

Through conscience man transcends the state and its laws and passes judgment on them. But even more, through conscience man transcends even his religion, and still more, dares to judge even God himself. It was thus that Abraham dared to question God about the justice of destroying Sodom, and Job could cry out:

> Behold, he will slay me; I have no hope;
> yet I will defend my ways to His face. (Job 13:15)

Religion may enhance or degrade man; it all depends on what it is. But without conscience, man has no dignity; without it, man is not man.

For those to whom conscience and religion are indissolubly intertwined, the Free Exercise Clause generally offers adequate protection. Congress, in exempting from military service men who claim conscientious objection to war on account of their *religious* training and belief, has, according to the Supreme Court, gone beyond the compulsion of the constitutional letter. But conscience that speaks to the heart, mind, and will of a man in words other than those he is willing to label "religious" finds no protection in the Free Exercise Clause, though it may receive some protection under the other freedoms guaranteed by the First Amendment: speech, press, assembly, and petition. But this is not true of the nonreligious conscientious objector. He has no standing at all under the law once the religious ground of his claim is removed from under him.

This is a defect. Not only in terms of the nonreligious pacifist, but also of religion; for, by insisting that conscience must speak as religion if it is to be heard in the legal forum, the law subtly offers inducements to conscience to express itself in certain ways and possibly even to color or falsify its assertions. This can have the effect of degrading religion, making of it a tool with which to achieve certain desired results not otherwise attainable.

Furthermore, if the religious person believes that religion is always rooted in conscience, it is conscience that is primary and religion that is derivative. Religion must honor conscience as a child honors its parents.

To protect religion fully, it is necessary to protect conscience, on which it is based and without which it could not long exist. One day the Supreme Court will feel itself compelled to recognize this fact and to give it constitutional dignity. The Court has held that the Constitution protects rights not expressly mentioned.[32] Recently the Court enumerated the following rights, which have been placed under the protection of the First Amendment because they fall within its spirit though not within its letter:

Freedom of association

The right to educate a child in a school of the parents' choice —public, private, parochial

The right to study a foreign language in a private school

The right to distribute, to receive, and to read printed matter

Freedom to teach

The right of privacy.

The Court has held that, without these "peripheral rights," the rights specifically enumerated in the Constitution would be less secure. The First Amendment has a "penumbra" in which these rights are protected.

In the same way the Court should conclude that in order to secure more fully the rights protected by the Free Exercise Clause, it is necessary to protect conscience even when it purports to speak in a language ostensibly nonreligious.

By seeing conscience in this light, the Court will avoid involvement in the insoluble problems generated by such indefinable terms as "religion," "religious," "atheism," "secularism," and "secular." These words no longer have the black-and-white pejorative or denotative meanings they once had. Religions are now facing the world and are committed to a this-world activist program; political ideologies like nationalism, Communism, and Americanism now very much act like religions and claim total commitment. Seditious utterances and blasphemy, loyalty and piety are no longer as different from each other as they once seemed to be.

These considerations make constitutional issues much more complex than they must have been even to such sophisticated men as Madison and Jefferson almost two centuries ago, and reinforce the insight:

Specific guarantees in the Bill of Rights have penumbras, formed by emanations from those guarantees that help give them life and substance.[33]

The case for the constitutional recognition of conscience is even stronger than for freedom of association and the other "emanations" recognized by the Court, for, as we have said, conscience is or has become the matrix and religion the emanation. It is conscience that today gives "life and substance" to religion.

Notes

I. The New Look of the Church-State Problem

1. *The Documents of Vatican II,* ed. W. M. Abbott (New York, 1966), pp. 120, 121.
2. Ibid., p. 362.
3. Ibid., p. 363.
4. Ibid., p. 125.
5. Ibid., p. 126.
6. Ibid., p. 127.
7. In 1967 there were 366 Jewish all-day schools with 75,000 pupils—about twelve per cent of the total enrollment in Jewish schools.
8. See data in Milton R. Konvitz, "Separation of Church and State: the First Freedom," 14 *Law and Contemporary Problems* 44 (1949).
9. Andrew M. Greeley and Peter H. Rossi, *The Education of Catholic Americans* (Chicago, 1966); *Catholic Schools in Action: The Notre Dame Study of Catholic Elementary and Secondary Education in the United States* (Notre Dame, 1966); Mary Perkins Ryan, *Are Parochial Schools the Answer?* (New York, 1964).
10. *Engel v. Vitale,* 370 U.S. 421 (1962); *Abington School District v. Schempp,* and *Murray v. Curlett,* 374 U.S. 203 (1963).
11. See Horace M. Kallen, "Secularism as a Religion," 4 *J. for Scientific Study of Religion* 145 (1965); Larry Shiner, "The

Concept of Secularization in Empirical Research," 6 *J. for Scientific Study of Religion* 207 (1967).

II. What Is Religion?

1. The description is based largely on Louis Adolphe Thiers, *History of the French Revolution* (Philadelphia, 1894), Vol. III. See also Franklin L. Baumer, *Religion and the Rise of Scepticism* (New York, 1960), Ch. I; D. G. Charlton, *Secular Religions in France 1815–1870* (London, 1963), Ch. I.

2. John Morley, *Miscellanies* (London, 1888), Vol. I, pp. 103–104.

3. Auguste A. Comte, *A General View of Positivism* (London, 2nd ed., 1880), p. 295.

4. John Stuart Mill, *Letters*, Vol. II, pp. 362–363.

5. Comte, op. cit., note 3, Ch. VI.

6. Basil Willey, *Nineteenth Century Studies* (London, 1949), p. 188.

7. *U.S. v. Reynolds*, 98 U.S. 148 (1878).

8. Cf. *Permoli v. New Orleans*, 3 How. (U.S.) 589 (1845).

9. Paul E. Freund and Robert Ulich, *Religion and the Public Schools* (Cambridge, 1965), p. 12.

10. *Davis v. Beason*, 133 U.S. 333 (1890).

11. *United States v. Macintosh*, 283 U.S. 605 (1931).

12. *United States v. Ballard*, 322 U.S. 78 (1944).

13. *Parker v. Commissioner of Internal Revenue*, 365 F.2d 792 (1966) (C.A.8th Circ.).

14. *Ginzburg v. United States*, 383 U.S. 463 (1966).

15. See *Henningsen v. Bloomfield Motors, Inc.*, 32 N.J. 358 (1960).

16. *Meinhard v. Salmon*, 249 N.Y. 458 (1928).

17. In re *Estate of Supple*, 55 Cal. Rpts. 542 (1966).

18. *Cantwell v. Conn.*, 310 U.S. 296, 310 (1940).

19. *United States v. Carolene Products Co.*, 304 U.S. 144, 152, note 4 (1938).

20. *N.A.A.C.P. v. Button*, 371 U.S. 415 (1963).

21. 4 Elliot's *Debates on the Federal Constitution* (1876), p. 571; quoted in *The New York Times* case at p. 271.

22. See *Sheldon v. Fannin*, 221 F. Supp. 766, at 775 (1963); *Kolbeck v. Kramer*, 202 A. 2d 889 (N.J. Super. Ct. 1964).

III. Religion and Secularism

1. *Everson v. Board of Education,* 330 U.S. 1(1947), opinion by Justice Black for the Court. On the issue of separation of church and state, or the meaning of the Establishment Clause, the Court was unanimous.
2. Bill for Establishing Religious Freedom, prepared by Jefferson for Virginia in 1779, and adopted in 1786. See Konvitz, *Fundamental Liberties of a Free People* (1957), p. 25.
3. Ibid., p. 280.
4. Leonard W. Levy, *Jefferson and Civil Liberties: The Darker Side* (1963), pp. 43–44, 171.
5. *Cincinnati v. Vester,* 281 U.S. 439 (1930).
6. *Watson v. Jones,* 13 Wall (U.S.) 679 (1872).
7. *Fellowship of Humanity v. County of Alameda,* 315 P.2d 394 (Calif. District Court of Appeal, 1957).
8. *Washington Ethical Society v. District of Columbia,* 294 F.2d 127 (1957).
9. *Torcaso v. Watkins,* 367 U.S. 488 (1961).
10. Morris R. Cohen, "Atheism," *Encycl. of the Soc. Sciences,* Vol. II, pp. 292–294. *The Documents of Vatican II,* Walter M. Abbott, gen. ed. (New York, 1966), 218 pp.
11. Anson Phelps Stokes and Leo Pfeffer, *Church and State in the United States* (1964), p. 529.
12. *The New York Times,* November 15, 1962.
13. Ibid., November 14, 1962.
14. Ibid., November 30, 1962.
15. *People v. Woody,* 394 P.2d 813 (1964).
16. *Leary v. United States,* 383 F.2d 851 (1967).
17. *The New York Times,* September 20, 1966; October 2, 1966.
18. Letter to Henry W. Rankin, quoted in Gay Wilson Allen, *William James* (1967), p. 425.
19. Ibid., p. 432.
20. Ibid., p. 466.
21. See *William James on Psychical Research,* edited by Gardner Murphy and Robert O. Ballou (1961), pp. 329–330.
22. "Psychedelics and Religion: A Symposium," by Allen Ginsberg and others, in *Humanist,* September–December 1967, p. 155.

23. Joseph Albo, *Sefer Ha-Ikkarim*. Translated by Isaac Husik (Philadelphia, 1929). Bk. I, Ch. 24.
24. *The Documents of Vatican II*, ed. Walter M. Abbott (New York, 1966), p. 347.
25. Ibid., pp. 662, 663.
26. Ibid., pp. 218–219.
27. James A. Pike, "The Right to Be an Atheist," *Coronet*, April 1961.
28. Locke, *Second Treatise of Civil Government and a Letter Concerning Toleration*, ed. J. W. Gough (London, 1947), p. 156.

IV. Conscience in the First Amendment

1. *Leary v. U.S.*, 383 F.2d 851 (1967).
2. *People v. Woody*, 394 P.2d 813 (1964).
3. *Reynolds v. U.S.*, 98 U.S. 145 (1878).
4. *Sherbert v. Verner*, 374 U.S. 398 (1963). The decision was seven to two, with Justices Harlan and White dissenting.
5. *U.S. News and World Report*, September 26, 1966, p. 90.
6. Joseph Albo, *Sefer Ha-Ikkarim*, Vol. I, Introduction by Isaac Husik, p. xix.
7. Ibid., p. 47.
8. Erasmus, *The Praise of Folly*, trans. by H. H. Hudson (Princeton, 1941), p. 78.
9. E.g., *Dennis v. U.S.* 341 U.S. 494 (1951); *Communist Party v. Subversive Activities Control Board*, 367 U.S. 1 (1961); *American Communications Assoc. v. Douds*, 339 U.S. 382 (1950).
10. See *Provisions of Federal Law Held Unconstitutional by the Supreme Court of the United States*, Library of Congress (U.S. Gov. Printing Office, 1936). See also *Trop v. Dulles*, 356 U.S. 86, at p. 104 (1958). From 1937 to 1958, the Court had declared seven federal statutes unconstitutional. There have been additional invalidations since then. The latest such decision was U.S. v. Robel, 88 S.Ct. 419 (Dec. 11, 1967).
11. Case cited supra note 4, p. 407.
12. John Stuart Mill, *On Liberty* (1859), ch. IV.
13. *The Heart of Emerson's Journal*, ed. Bliss Perry (Boston, 1926), pp. 49, 50.

14. *The Heart of Thoreau's Journal*, ed. Odell Shepard (Boston, 1927), pp. 304, 336.
15. *The Adams-Jefferson Letters*, ed. L. J. Cappon (Chapel Hill, 1959), Vol. II, pp. 506, 512.
16. Jefferson letter to Edward Dowse, 1803.
17. Cf. Konvitz, "Privacy and the Law: a Philosophical Prelude," 31 *Law and Contemporary Problems* 272 (spring 1966).
18. *U.S. v. Seeger*, 380 U.S. 163 (1965).
19. 50 U.S. Code, appendix § 456(j), 1964.
20. *U.S. v. Macintosh*, 283 U.S. 605, 633, 634 (1931).
21. Stone, "The Conscientious Objector," 21 *Columbia Univ. L. Q.* 253 (1919).
22. For an anticipation of this line of argument, see Konvitz, "The Meaning of 'Religion' in the First Amendment: The Torcaso Case," in *The Catholic World*, August 1963.
23. See *U.S. v. Macintosh*, 283 U.S. 605 (1931), at 623.
24. "Notes on Locke and Shaftesbury," *The Papers of Thomas Jefferson*, ed. Julian P. Boyd (Princeton, 1960), Vol. I, p. 547.
25. A case of a Jehovah's Witness: *Riles v. U.S.* 223 F.2d 786 (1955). A case of one who took his stand on vegetarianism: *Tamarkin v. U.S.*, 260 F.2d 436; cert. den. 359 U.S. 925; reh. den. 359 U.S. 976 (1958).
26. *Documents of Vatican II*, ed. W.M. Abbott (New York, 1966), pp. 213–214.
27. Ibid., p. 292.
28. Ibid., p. 292.
29. See Eric D'Arcy, *Conscience and Its Right to Freedom* (New York, 1961), pp. 87 ff. See also A. F. Carrillo de Albornoz, *Religious Liberty* (New York, 1967), pp. 42, 51, 61, 118, 138, 140; John Courtney Murray, ed., *Religious Liberty: An End and a Beginning* (New York, 1966), pp. 24–25.
30. Op. cit. supra, note 26, p. 213.
31. John Henry Newman, *A Letter Addressed to His Grace the Duke of Norfolk on the Occasion of Mr. Gladstone's Recent Expostulation* (1875), pp. 53 ff.
32. *Griswold v. Conn.*, 381 U.S. 479 (1965).
33. Ibid., p. 484.

Index